# Trauma Informed
# Directed Sandplay

Dr Patricia Sherwood

National Library of Australia Cataloguing-in-Publication entry

Author: Dr Sherwood, Patricia

Title: Trauma informed Directed Sandplay

ISBN: 978-0-9876143-9-1

Publisher: by Sophia Publications 2020

Subjects: Counselling, Psychology, Art therapy

All case studies in this book are composites and do not relate to any one person.

DISCLAIMER

While every care has been taken in researching and compiling the information in this book, it is in no way intended to replace professional medical advice and counselling. Readers are encouraged to seek such help as they deem necessary. The author and publisher specifically disclaim any liability arising from the application of information in this book.

Layout and design by Tuck Loon

Cover picture: Courtesy of Michael Horsely.

## Dedication

To the staff at Accordwest, especially Nicole
for her inspirational leadership and
to Jaqui, Mike, Syd and Naomi for their unfaltering commitment
and compassion in creating a trauma informed sanctuary
for our clients.

# Acknowledgements

To Gomathi whose encouragement to document my trauma informed sandplay training resulted in this book. Without her encouragement this book would never have been birthed.

To Rosemary Kroll for kindly documenting some sequences while I was training. To Janet for her endless dedication to editing and proofing the manuscript.

And especially to my clients, without whom none of this knowledge would have been possible and who continue to demonstrate the incredible capacity of the human spirit to seek healing even in the face of traumatic experiences.

# Contents

# Introduction

*"Traumatized people chronically feel unsafe inside their bodies: The past is alive in the form of gnawing interior discomfort. Their bodies are constantly bombarded by visceral warning signs, and, in an attempt to create awareness of what is played out inside, they learn to hide from their selves."*

Bessel A. Van der Kolk, (2015, p.97)

It is now well established through research that trauma is stored in the right side of the brain, the non verbal side where the language is not words, but sounds, smells, symbols, tactile, kinaesthetic sensations and visual imagery (Schiffer, Teicher & Papanicolaou, 1995...). Zoja (2011, p.32) elucidates why talk therapy is inadequate to deal with traumatised clients:

> "...the dreaded flashbacks that people experience are psycho-physical states of being connected to mental images. Psychological intervention relying entirely on verbal expression would never be able to reach the emotions connected with such experiences."

The connection between art therapy, trauma recovery and neuro-science has been established as positive by Belkofer and Konopka, (2003) and Kruk (2004) cited in Klorer (2005, p.218). Art therapies such as sandplay, by connecting the unconscious feelings with conscious thinking can produce new integration in the psyche that reduces post traumatic stress disorder (PTSD) and other traumatic states such as combat related PTSD (Malichiodi, 2016; Read Johnson, 1987).

Sandplay provides a method for facilitating the integration of trauma and provides a bridge that enables assimilation into the client's conscious and verbal world. It offers a contained healing space where that which is hidden in the psyche can be revealed. Sandplay therapy has been widely used to work with clients suffering from a diversity of traumatic experiences. Tornero and Capella (2017) report on its potential for working with children that have been sexually abused. Freedle, Altschul and Freedle (2015) note how sandplay positively impacted engagement in treatment with youth suffering from co-occurring substance use disorders and trauma. Results demonstrated improved daily functioning at home and school, and reduced the severity of their substance addiction.

Trauma is not simply an emotionally troublesome or disturbing experience. Rather it can be defined as a response to a threat perceived as life-threatening. Trauma is the result of an experience that attacks the very essence of the human being's capacity to survive physically, mentally, and emotionally. This profoundly affects the emergent self, particularly in young children. In order to survive, the child/person dissociates, that is splits off their awareness from the life-threatening experience by either "disappearing" into a part of the body and retreating from contact with the real physical world, or "excarnating" more commonly known as dissociation. This occurs when a person experiences their conscious mind leaving the physical body and entering into another dimension of experience detached from the physical reality. These basic survival strategies in the face of trauma are documented in detail by Sherwood (2010, pp136-141). This separation results in unknown, disowned parts of the psyche, split off from the conscious self which when triggered by sensory similarities to the original experience, result in flashbacks, hallucinations, and panic attacks. These experiences when combined produce PTSD (post traumatic stress disorder) which profoundly interrupts the person's capacity to relate fully and accurately to the present moment (Read-Johnson, 1987). Neuro psychiatry is providing clear evidence that traumatic attachment histories affect the frontolimbic parts of the brain (Shore, 2002). In particular, they retard the development of the right cortical areas that are involved in emotional regulation so that sudden rages and anger outbursts without provocations understood by others, may possess the child or adolescent even when they are in a nonthreatening and safe environment. Van Der Kolk (2014, p.91) in his remarkable book: *The Body keeps the score: brain, mind and body in the healing of trauma*, documents the profound impairments that trauma causes in the functioning of the brain:

> ...the scans of the eighteen chronic PTSD patients with severe early-life trauma was startling. There was almost no activation of any of the self-sensing areas of the brain: The MPFC, the anterior cingulate, the parietal cortex, and the insula did not light up at all; the only area that showed a slight activation was the posterior cingulate, which is responsible for basic orientation in space. There could be only one explanation for such results: In response to the trauma itself, and in coping with the dread that persisted long afterward, these patients had learned to shut down the brain areas that transmit the visceral feelings and emotions that accompany and define terror. Yet in everyday life, those same brain areas are responsible for registering the entire range of emotions and sensations that form the foundation of our self-awareness...

Recognizing the impact of trauma on the profound structures of the psyche, service providers should create a system of service delivery and psychotherapeutic interventions that are trauma-informed. These will have the following characteristics. This system and approach will realize the widespread impact of trauma on the individual's life, recognise the symptoms of trauma upon the client and family system, and respond by integrating this awareness into practices, interventions and service delivery. There will be a commitment to avoid re-traumatising the client in the recovery process. The Orygen Centre (2018) identifies the five central components of trauma informed interventions which are:

1. working safely to avoid re-traumatisation,

2. conducting a trauma sensitive assessment,

3. developing a shared understanding of the impacts of the trauma on their presenting issues and problems

4. providing psycho-education

5. working in a strengths based way with young people and their families/carers to support recovery.

Sandplay therapy has a long history of working with trauma effectively. First developed by Dora Kalff in 1956, it has spawned many different approaches. Central though to all approaches is the use of the sand box which provides a safe, non-verbal, contained space for the client to use figurines through which they can express their inner experiences. It also gives them the opportunity to re-create and transform these traumatic experiences through their own agency. Zappacosta (2013) notes how sandplay therapy provides a unique model of containment for trauma within the parameters of the sandtray itself, within the trust built up in the therapeutic relationship and within the safe and contained setting of the therapy room. Kalff emphasised the safe and supportive space provided by sandplay. She often saw her clients over many sessions documenting how the psyche was gradually working toward integration of traumatic experiences through the many trays the client completed and she observed. This is known as the classical sandtray therapy. It is a spontaneous, undirected process. However, there has also developed a range of directed sandplay processes where the therapists suggest to the client certain processes as documented in the work of Boik & Goodwin (2000) and Pearson and Wilson, (2001).

In this book I provide detailed, directed sequences for use in sandplay therapy that are trauma informed and particularly appropriate for adolescents and adults. They can be adapted for older children that have reached formal operational or abstract thinking, usually around eleven years onwards. Some of the sequences are appropriate for concrete operational thinkers, usually children between eight and eleven years of age. They are not suitable for pre-operational thinkers or young children who do not live in a world governed by logic or process. With young traumatised children it seems that spontaneous sandplay remains most effective for their experiences allowing them entirely to express through catharsis, integration and renewal their traumatic experiences using symbol and story. These directed sandplay sequences however, have been developed to facilitate the process of integration and catharsis of repressed traumatic experiences, and trialled and implemented with many hundreds of youth and adults. Their experiential efficacy is evident in the diminution or disappearance of the presenting problem in the cases of self harm, in particular cutting, OCD , body dysmorphia, selective mutism, and anorexia which are the focus of this book. There are also included some directed sequences to assist in the working with addiction, suicide ideation and recovery from divorce which facilitate the client's resilience to deal more effectively with these issues.

Essentially, the model of directed sandtray outlined in this book, is based on a somatic model of psychotherapy which assumes trauma is a bodily experience and that it is stored deeply in the body cells requiring therapy that is bodily focused, and sandplay can be used as an artistic medium to facilitate this bodily process. Unless the body experiences new sensations through touching and moving the sand

and the pieces, new imagery through the richness of the provided symbols within a new environment of peace which means a warm, non judgemental, authentic therapist, the body is unable to re-energise and re-program the bodily cells with new information. That which is stored in the body, for example, the emotional debri of a traumatised childhood and reflected in the brain, needs body-mind interventions to heal and transform. The quick solution is to deal pharmacologically with the acute bodily experiences of trauma but this overlooks and ignores the cycle between body-mind and the need to integrate both with conscious awareness. Zoja (2011, p.44) describes this dynamic and interventions powerfully:

> The traumatic experience is deeply ingrained in the body. It can be roughly made out in sores and hardened muscles, and physiologically detected in a change of blood parameters, synaptic connections in the brain, cerebral volume and a whole row of metabolic processes which are in turn related to hormonal and endocrinological regulatory circuits... (this) has increased the tendency to proceed only according to a medical model, thereby overlooking psychodynamic connections and their interaction with physiological ones.

Increasingly in clinical practice, I see traumatised children from three years into adolescence and adulthood, who have been treated only pharmacologically with anti-anxiety, anti-depressant and anti-psychotic medications for their anxiety, anger, low moods, poor concentration and sensory inadequacies. The long term adverse side-effects of these medications on young developing bodies and minds, should alert us to the hazards of attempting pharmacological interventions only (Breggin, 2000, 1998). In children from traumatic backgrounds, the minimum intervention should involve a combination of pharmacological and psychotherapeutic interventions, preferably commencing with counselling first, prior to mental health medication. Medication is too easy to apply as a quick, short term fix, but likely to be a long term liability to the health of the traumatised child. More significantly it removes agency from the client, who too readily can enter the role of the victim unable and or unwilling to take any action to improve their life. This state of victimhood is so poignantly captured by Van der Kolk (2014,p.216):

> When we ignore these quintessential dimensions of humanity, we deprive people of ways to heal from trauma and restore their autonomy. Being a patient, rather than a participant in one's healing process, separates suffering people from their community and alienates them from an inner sense of self. It is essential for healing that traumatised clients experience the restoration of trusting relationships with self, others and the world around them. It is through positive sensory experiences, embracing appropriate client centred movement, breathing, colour, sound, imagery and touch that one can support clients to facilitate their healing. Safe touch is the first and most elementary way of calming down because first and foremost we need to feel safe in our own skin and our own sensory world.

It is because of this desire to increase the health and well being of traumatised children and adolescents that these directed sandplay sequences have been developed and documented. The sequences, while based on the client's experience, are also empirical in that they provide repeatable sequences for practitioners that are controlled, directed, rational, and intersubjectively verifiable. These sequences have a number of repeatable steps, usually three to five and can be conducted by the therapist. Once mastered these sandplay sequences can be applied across a range of clients in a diversity of situations, with similar presenting issues. As a result of using these sequences, clients have achieved positive outcomes quickly, kindly and effectively and experienced release from their traumatic burden. It has taken much encouragement and prompting both from my colleagues and students in training, to convince me to document these sandplay sequences because they have observed their efficacy with clients. While traditional sandplay therapists may find these disturbingly contaminated by the 21st century's need for efficacy and speed, these directed sandplay sequences were developed consciously, after observing many thousands of cases of trauma induced mental health conditions and the psychic structures that underpin them.

Finally it is NOT recommended that these sandplay sequences be used immediately with traumatized clients. It is essential that initially the client has a safe space to spontaneously explore the traumas in their life through non directed sandplay. However, once the client has established confidence in the sandplay environment, and including a trusting relationship with the therapist, then these directed and structured sandplay sequences can be extremely beneficial. They enable clients, particularly once they have reached adolescence, to develop insight and resources that facilitate the healing potential within themselves through the sandplay sequences. They tend to speed up the process of transformation and for those of us working under the limits of the ten sessions per year Medicare counselling rebate services, it is most helpful to maximise the time and resources available to us. Sandplay provides a splendid opportunity to work deeply and profoundly, so that the invisible may be made visible, the intangible be made tangible and the unknowable be made knowable. Communication, first with self, is the traumatised client's life-line back to humanity. Trauma is socially induced and must be socially recovered so the client is no longer held prisoner in their own pain. When witnessed, this becomes our pain at the inadequacies of our social world to provide healthy opportunities for all people. Trauma shared with another caring human being who has the skills to support and empower the sufferer provides a great step towards healing.

As Bernock (2019) expounds: "Trauma is personal. It does not disappear if it is not validated. When it is ignored or invalidated the silent screams continue internally heard only by the one held captive."

## REFERENCES

Bernock, D., (2019) Emerging With Wings: A True Story of Lies, Pain, And The LOVE that Heals https://www.goodreads.com/quotes/tag/trauma?page=2 Accessed 24-12-2019.

Boik, B., & Goodwin, E., (2000) *Sandplay therapy: a step by step manual for psychotherapists of diverse orientations.* N.Y.: Norton & Co.

Breggin, P. (2000) *Reclaiming our children*, N.Y.: Perseus books.

Breggin, P. & Breggin, G. (1998) *The war against children of colour* Maine: Common Courage Press.

Freedle, L., Altschul, D., Freedle, A. (2015) The role of sandplay therapy in the treatment of adolescents and young adults with co-occurring substance use disorders and trauma. In *Journal of sandplay therapy* 24(2) 127-145.

Kallf, D. (2003) Sandplay: a psychotherapeutic approach to the psyche. CA: Temenos Press.

Klorer, P. (2005) Expressive therapy with severely maltreated children: neuroscience contributions. Art therapy. In *The Journal of the American Art Therapy Association* 22(4) pp.213-220.

Malichiodi, C. (2016) *Art therapy: treating combat related PTSD* accessed

21-12-2019 https://www.psychologytoday.com/au/blog/arts-and-health/201610/art-therapy-treating-combat-related-ptsd

Orygen (2018) *Clinical practice in youth mental health.* What is trauma-informed care and how is it implemented in youth healthcare settings? https://www.orygen.org.au/Search-Result?searchtext=wht+is+traumainformed+care+and+how+is+it+implemented+in+youth+healthcare+settings%3f&searchmode=anyword  Accessed 23-12-2019

Pearson, M & Wilson, H (2019) Sandplay Therapy; a safe, creative space for trauma recovery. In *Australian Counselling Research Journal* ISSN 1832-1135

Pearson, M & Wilson, H (2001) *Sandplay and symbol work. Emotional healing and personal development with children, adolescents and adults.* Melbourne: Acer.

Read Johnson, D. (1987) The role of the creative arts therapies in the diagnosis and treatment of psychological trauma. In *Pergammon Journals* 14. pp7-13.

Schiffer, F., Teicher, M., & Papanicolaou, A. (1995) Evoked potential evidence for right brain activity during the recall of traumatic memories. In *Journal of Neuropsychiatry and Clinical neurosciences,* 7(2), 169-175.doi.10.1176/jnp.7.2.169

Sherwood, P. (2010) *Holistic Counselling: a new vision for mental health.* Bunbury, Sophia Publications.

Shore, A. (2002) Dysregulation of the right brain: A fundamental mechanism of traumatic attachment and the psychopathogensis of post traumatic stress disorder. In *Australian and New Zealand Journal of Psychiatry,* 36, pp.9-30.

Tornero, M., & Capella, C., (2017) Change during Psychotherapy through sandplay in children that have been sexually abused. In *Front psychology* 2017 May 4 doi: 10.3389/fpsyg.2017.00617

Van der Kolk, Bessell  (2014) *The Body Keeps the Score: Brain, Mind, and Body in the Healing of Trauma.*  N.Y.Viking.

Van der Kolk, Bessell  (2019) *The Body Keeps the Score: Brain, Mind, and Body in the Healing of Trauma.* https://www.goodreads.com/work/quotes/26542319-the-body-keeps-the-score-brain-mind-and-body-in-the-healing-of-trauma   Accessed 26-12-2019.

Zappocosta S. (2013) Sandplay therapy: a way of rediscovering inner wisdom in the body and psyche. In S. Loue (ed) *Expressive therapies for sexual issues*  pp.181-199. N.Y.: Springer.

Zoja, Eva Pattis (2011) *Sandplay Therapy in Vulnerable Communities.* London: Routledge.

# CHAPTER 1
# Self harm through cutting

*"There are wounds that never show on the body that are deeper and more hurtful than anything that bleeds."*

Laurell K. Hamilton (2019)

Non-suicidal self-injury (NSSI) is of epidemic proportions among adolescents in the western world and the most common form of self-injury is cutting but may also include burning, bruising, hair pulling or hitting oneself. Each year, one in five females and one in seven males engage in self-injury. It is a popular peer group dysfunctional behaviour to manage unresolved trauma and stress. Adolescent peers share techniques and photos, and develop a sub-culture of cutting in many schools. Over sixty per cent of cutters are females. Research has shown that fifty percent of those who self-injure are sexual abuse victims (Gluck, 2012). The prevalence of trauma among self harm cutters includes abuse in childhood, addiction, PTSD, and depression. It is often triggered by a recent difficult life event such as the breakup of a relationship, conflict with parental figures, particularly the mother, school failures, bullying, and recent episodes of violence or rejection by significant others. (https://www.lifeline. org.au/get-help/topics/self-harm). Cutting is most prevalent among female adolescents in Australia and an online survey (Murray, Warm & Fox 2005) reveals a profile of an adolescent who is female with a history of sexual and or physical abuse and who often has an eating disorder as well. She cuts her arms and legs on a daily or weekly basis. This person usually hides cutting implements, scars and bleeding from significant others such as carers, parents and other authority figures. However, she may publically display it through photographs to selected peers who also cut.

When working with clients that self harm the following explanations are common. "Cutting helps me get rid of bad blood and bad family history", "it releases my anxiety or tension", "relieves my feelings of loneliness and rejection", "relieves my negative feelings of failure" or "fear of failure", "helps me cope with self-blame and hopelessness" and "gives me a feeling of control over these overwhelming feelings". It is common to hear that "Cutting also helps me focus on the pain in my body and forget the pain of all the negative bad feelings in my life". Adolescent cutters also state that they find camaraderie, support and acceptance with other cutters who understand them and their problems in a way that the adults and people around them do not. Unfortunately however, cutting is a negative strategy for expressing negative emotions and forms a body-mind pathway that reinforces it as a way of relieving emotional stress.  This relief circuit becomes harder and harder to break the more frequently cutting is used as the means to release tension and trauma (Hemmen, 2019).

Cutting should be perceived as a coping strategy masking much deeper traumatic experiences. It is adopted by teens in particular, as they often lack the skills and experience to develop better coping mechanisms and their family, community and/or school environments fail to model and educate alternative ways for coping with stress, disappointment and perceived failures. Usually when the adolescents present in therapy for cutting themselves, it has come to the notice of the school or parents despite the secretiveness of most cutters around concerned adults. By the time that it comes to a concerned adult's attention, it is usually a habitual pattern of dealing with overwhelming negative feelings, so it is challenging for the therapist and client especially if the client believes it is the best and only way to deal with their stressors and adults simply don't understand. Once the therapist has established rapport with the adolescent through some spontaneous, undirected sandplays and conversations, one can begin to introduce directed sandplay sequences. The first of these directed sequences is an orientation sequence to facilitate the client's understanding of the stages of the cutting process.

## 1. Sandtray sequence for exposing the client's experiential process of cutting

Although adolescents talk a great deal about their cutting escapades to each other, photograph it and circulate it via their mobile phones, they do not have an in depth understanding as to what drives the process, nor its costs to their health, nor interventions that they could make to prevent themselves engaging in the process. This first exercise is directed at exposing the negative cognitive distortions that drive the process.

The client is invited to choose objects from a diverse variety of figurines, both positive and negative, and place them from left to right along the horizontal middle line of the sandtray as follows:

### Step 1

- Ask the client to choose a piece to represent their feelings when they have the first thoughts about wanting to cut and then to place it in the sand tray. For example: "I am bad and a failure because I failed the maths test today". It is placed in the middle of the tray on the far left and labelled, "The "unhappy powerless one" or "sad or bad one" based on client's choice.

### Step 2

- Invite the client to choose a piece for the sand tray which represents how they feel and think when they are preparing to cut: for example "I am hopeless and I feel anxious". It is placed in the tray next to the last piece going across the tray from left to right and labelled, the "anxious one" or whatever they have said they are feeling.

## Step 3

- Ask the client to choose a piece that represents how they feel at the moment of cutting: It is placed in the tray next to the last piece going across the tray and labelled by the client. Usually they choose something like "I am powerful" or "I am in control".

## Step 4

- Ask the client to choose a piece that represents how they feel immediately after cutting. It is placed in the tray next to the last piece going across the tray and labelled by the client. Usually they choose something like "I am relieved" or "I feel calm."

## Step 5

- Invite the client to choose a piece to represent how they feel in the longer term after cutting. It is placed in the tray next to the last piece going across the tray and labelled by the client. Usually they choose something like "I regret it" or "I feel ashamed" or "I will be in trouble."

## Step 6

- Invite the client to reflect their feelings and thoughts at each of the points above. Work with the presenting trigger and the thoughts at each stage to elucidate with the client the cognitions and emotions that run that phase. After completion of the above steps, provide the client with insights which facilitate the client reframing their experiences during the process, into a positive way of thinking that moves them from victim to agent of change, from self-condemnation to self-compassion.

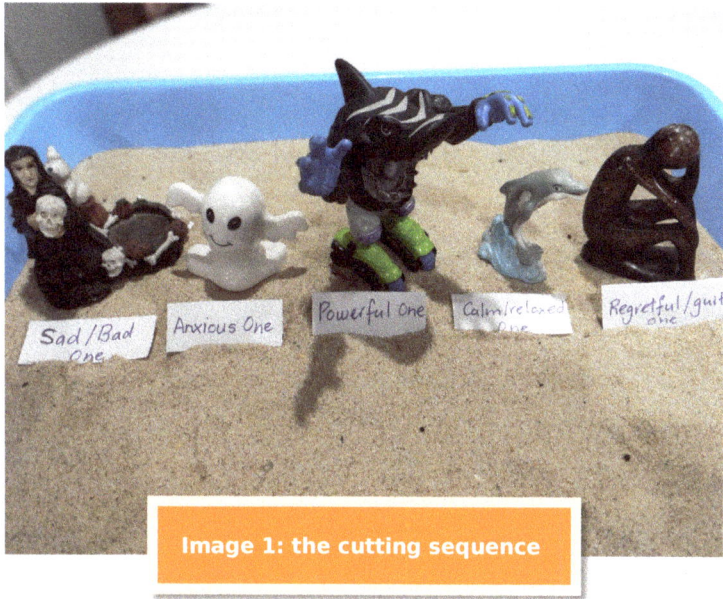

Image 1: the cutting sequence

**Reflection:**

Spend time with the client reflecting on the steps of the cutting sequence and create a conversational space for the client if they wish to share experiences, or comment on the above. Once a trusting nonjudgmental relationship is established with the client who is cutting, they are usually quite keen to share their experiences of cutting. Out of this conversation usually the second directed sandplay sequence will arise either in the same or next counselling session.

## 2. Sequence exposing the experiences that move the sad/bad and anxious one to cutting

**Step 1**

- Ask the client to write down all the bad feelings they have about themselves when feeling bad/ sad or anxious and before they resort to cutting.

**Step 2:**

- Select further pieces to represent the sad/bad one and the anxious one.

**Step 3:**

- Select pieces to represent these feelings and place around the sad/bad one and the anxious one.

- Label each piece so easily identifiable.

Image 2: the feelings of the sad/bad one that led to cutting

**Reflections**

In reflection with client help them to identify the trigger incidents in the client's experience that lead to each of these feelings. Work with the trigger incidents individually over as many sessions as required to explore further in sandplays how each one of these trigger feelings operate in the client's life. Use a range of additional techniques to transform these negative feelings based upon one's particular clinical therapeutic model.

**Interventions:**

As a holistic somatic therapist, (Sherwood, 2010) I would undertake the following process for each of the negative qualities they have placed in the above sandplay:

1.  Find where precisely in their body they feel the tension when speaking about a specific experience of one of their negative feelings eg. Loneliness

2.  Sense into this place and draw the shape of the tension

3.  Step into this place in the full body gesture of the shape you have drawn

4.  Recall the earliest memory of sensing your body in this shape and the associated feelings

5.  Do you feel attacked or abandoned? In the case of feeling loneliness, the most likely response is the feeling of abandonment.

6.  Proceed to resource the lonely one using sandplay or colour or movement or music depending on the client's preference and breathe back the antidote to the negative feeling. For example, encourage the client to breathe warmth and love, into their body (Sherwood 2010: p.108-109).

7.  Exercises to embody this new feeling of warmth and love would include suggesting and sometimes facilitating post session activities such as engaging in sports, hobbies, and social groups where the client can have the bodily experience of the required positive qualities on a regular basis. Usually these qualities have not been present in their daily lives or the client has felt unable to access them for some reason or the other.

8.  If the client experienced being attacked as well as abandoned then one would remove the force of the attack using somatic processes identified in Sherwood (2010 p.141-146) and implement boundary exercises. This involves the client finding how they feel attacked

and then using sound and "gesture removing" the force of the attack by the client repelling it with a loud "d" or "b" or "g".

Once having addressed over a number of sessions the qualities identified in the sandplay above, then I would proceed to the following directed sand play.

### 3. Sandplay sequence for resourcing the sad/bad one ( or however described) with required qualities

**Step 1:**

- Invite the client to select pieces to represent the bad/sad one and the anxious one and to place these figurines in the tray.

**Step 2:**

- Ask the client to select pieces that represent qualities that could provide sufficient support to the unhappy sad/bad one and the anxious one, so that they would not need to progress to the powerful cutting one but could go direct to the calm relaxed one.

- Place these pieces around the two suffering figures and label these pieces with their qualities.

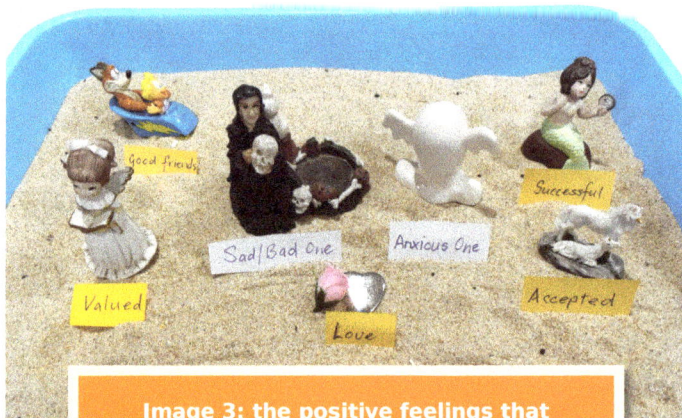

Image 3: the positive feelings that prevent cutting

**Reflection:** Discuss the implications of these qualities for the client's life. Follow up by a conversation with the client about the identified new qualities that need to come into their life in order for them not to need to progress to cutting themselves, and in order for the client to feel powerful and in control of their life. This will involve a number of internal changes for the client's thinking life as well as external changes such as networking, support mentoring, establishing new opportunities in social, sporting or educational contexts. Work with each of the qualities in the sandtray so as to create a space for the client to embody each quality in their lives through a particular activity. Engage family, school and other support networks for the client when and where required. Invite the client to photograph the sandtray containing these new possibilities and to refer to it regularly, at least for 7 days following the intervention.

Guilt, self-recrimination and regret are common post cutting experiences of clients, particularly when they are discovered by a significant other person such as a parent or school teacher. Clients who cut often go to great lengths to conceal their cutting activities by wearing long pants, armbands, wrist bands, long sleeved shirt and the like. Self-judgment keeps the vicious cycle going of failure and unworthiness that fuels the cutting experience. In order to break this cycle, a self-forgiveness sandplay process is implemented.

## 4. Sandplay: creating self-forgiveness sequence

**Step 1:**

Invite the client to place the regretful guilty one in the centre of the tray.

**Step 2:**

Ask the client to select four pieces that represent persons, archetypes or animals that could forgive them.

**Step 3:**

Request that the client place these around the guilty, regretful one and breathe in the quality of self forgiveness that they experience as receiving from these figures who they know have forgiven them and which they recognise as having an abundance of self-forgiveness.

**Step 4:**

Replace the regretful guilty figure which was in the centre of the sandtray with the self-accepting happy figure.

Photograph the completed sequence as a reminder of the resources for self acceptance that they can access in their life.

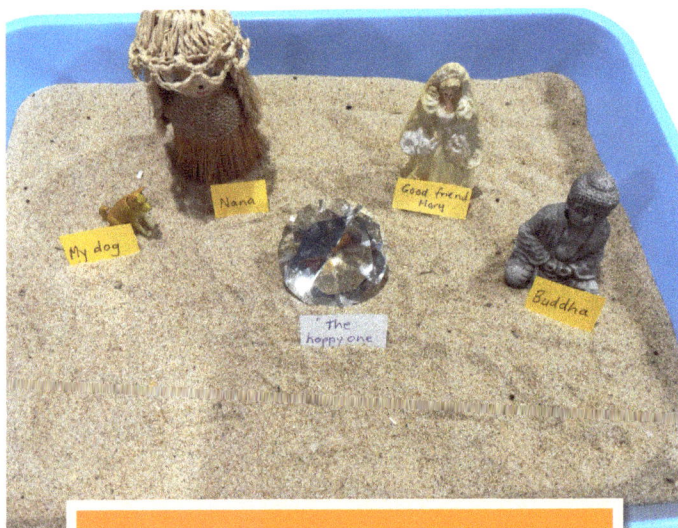

Image 4: finding self-acceptance and self-forgiveness

**Reflection:**

Open a conversational space for the client to share experiences of self-forgiveness and the challenges they experience in entering into this feeling. Enlarge the opportunities for the client to experience contact with the images that provide acceptance and forgiveness.

With clients who are cutting, the focus must be to transform the feelings of failure, anxiety, rejection, aloneness, unworthiness and powerlessness that drive this self-destructive process. Sandplay sequences can provide powerful pictures to assist the client to gain insight into this destructive process and to create new avenues of imagery and pathways to action. Combined with embodied strategies that change behaviours in their lives, and which are well documented in Sherwood (2013) and which include a range of expressive therapies such a music, art making, equine therapy, pet therapy as well as mindfulness meditation, these create new avenues open for personal growth and healing. The heart of all of these activities is building self-esteem, self-confidence and self-acceptance.

## REFERENCES

Gluck, S. (2012, August 24). *Self Injury, Self Harm Statistics and Facts, Healthy Place.* Retrieved on 2019, December 23 from https://www.healthyplace.com/abuse/self-injury/self-injury-self-harm-statistics-and-facts

Hamilton, L.K. (2019) *Mistral's Kiss*  https://www.goodreads.com/quotes/tag/trauma Accessed 24-12-2019.

Hemmen, Lucy (2019) https://www.psychologytoday.com/au/blog/teen-girls-crash-course/201211/stressed-out-teen-girls-cutting-cope (accessed the 24-12-19).

 Murray, C.,  Warm, A.,  & Fox, J.  (2005) An internet survey of adolescent self-injurers. In *Australian e-Journal for the Advancement of Mental Health (AeJAMH),* 4 (1) 2005. https://www.researchgate.net/

profile/Craig_Murray2/publication/238491296_An_Internet_survey_
of_adolescent_self-injurers/links/54d4c85c0cf2970e4e63a15f.pdf (
accessed 24-12-2019)

https://www.lifeline.org.au/get-help/topics/self-harm (accessed
24-12-19)

Sherwood, P. (2013) *Emotional Literacy for Adolescent Mental Health*
Melbourne: ACER.

Sherwood, P. (2010) *Holistic Counselling: a new vision for mental health.*
Bunbury, Sophia Publications.

# CHAPTER 2

# Anorexia

*"Trauma is personal. It does not disappear if it is not validated.*
*When it is ignored or invalidated the silent screams continue*
*internally heard only by the one held captive.*
*When someone enters the pain and hears the screams healing can begin."*

Bernock, D. (2019)

A norexia nervosa is an eating disorder whereby the person suffering from it believes that they are chronically overweight and will starve themselves or drastically reduce food intake in order to lose weight. It has two stages in my clinical experience. During stage one, the client knows that they are not overweight and that they are in the grip of the control of a voice that drives them irrationally to control their eating and to lose weight. During stage two, the client is seriously underweight, suffering from acute malnutrition but believes that they are overweight. They cannot enter into or respond to rational thought and will continue to starve themselves. Without external intervention, they may starve themselves even unto death. It primarily affects females and starts in adolescence, although the most seriously ill are between 20 and 45 years of age. It is found in approximately 0.5% of the population and it has the highest death rate of any mental illness at 20% of those afflicted with the illness (Australian Government Department of Health, 2005).

Anorexia is a complex psycho-social physical illness that has a cluster of emotional states underlying it. Mantilla, Norring, & Birgegard,

(2019) in their research identified self-image as the single most important predictor of becoming, remaining or ceasing to suffer from an eating disorder. The client's resilience and ability to overcome the disorder was directly correlated positively with the level of a client's self-love and low levels of self-blame and self judgment. Several research findings indicate that anorexic sufferers have high levels of body dissatisfaction, and that perfectionism, negative thoughts and emotions were highly correlated with body image distortion (Waldman, Loomes, Mountford, & Tchanturia, 2013). Perfectionism is identified as one of the key, if not central dysfunctional cognitive/ affective pattern in anorexia nervosa and often precludes effective treatment, encourages relapse and keeps the client in a chronic cycle of low self-esteem and critical self-judgement. (Hurst, 2013).

The impact of family systems upon the treatment of anorexia nervosa was well established by the Milan therapists in the 1970s and thoroughly documented by  Palazzoli-Selvini (1989,1978) who led a team of family therapists to identify  the dysfunctional patterns that families engage in that lead a family member to become anorexic. Using a systemic approach and challenging the family system scripts and communication patterns, the Milan therapists had extraordinary success in reducing anorexia in the sufferer within the family system. More recently a modified family based treatment (FBT) at the Maudsley centre is showing good prognosis for long term successful outcomes

While it is clear that anorexia is a very complex phenomena and that clinical psychotherapeutic treatments can contribute significantly towards amelioration of the disorder, medical intervention may often be required particularly in more chronic or acute cases. The following sections of this chapter present sandplay sequences which have been found to be effective in curtailing the eating disorder. This is particularly so when it is in the initial stage, while the sufferer still demonstrates the capacity for reason and insight.

## 1. Sandplay sequence for revealing the core dynamic of the thought directing the self-starvation.

The basic strategy in working with clients suffering from anorexia is to begin with some undirected spontaneous sandplays to see what emerges from the client's experience, identify where they are in their life journey, as well as build a therapeutic relationship that is open, warm and encouraging. Giving the client time and space to feel in control of the therapeutic process is an important first step with such clients. Once this sense of safety and ease has been established with the client, the therapist can begin with the following trauma informed directed sandplay.

**Step1:**

- Invite the client to select a piece that represents their physical body and place it in the centre of the sandplay.

- Ask the client to reflect on the state of their physical body. Why have they chosen the particular piece they have to represent their physical body? This is very revealing.

**Step 2:**

- Invite the client to choose a piece that represents their human spirit, the best of whom they can potentially be and who represents their highest and most creative potential. One may call this their "I" or highest self potential, the insightful part of themselves. One may ask the client to label it as such and place the piece on the right of the piece representing their body. Then with the client, reflect on their best potential, not yet manifest but latent within themselves, their dreams of who they could be in the world and how they could bring their own unique light to the world in their own way. Here the therapist can build with the client a vision of health, self-acceptance and positivity which increases their motivation.

## Step 3:

- Ask the client to select a piece that represents "the thought" that tells them that they must not eat, that they are fat and direct them to place it on the left side of the piece representing their physical body. It is "the thought" that tells them that they are not good enough and that they are a failure but if they don't eat they will feel better, more in control and less of a failure. Invite the client to elucidate the specific message "the negative thought" contains and the "deal" between the "negative thought" and themself. This deal usually promises relief from bad feelings of low self-worth, failure, and their inability to meet external standards. In exchange though, the deal includes the clause that the client must not eat.

- Label this voice "the oppositional I" because it opposes their "I" on the right side of the sandtray and is working to prevent it coming into being. Explain to the client that there is a war going on between the "I" and the "Oppositional I" for control of the client's body which is the centre piece in the tray. Encourage the client to reflect on this war for control of their body and to share their experiences.

Image 5: "I" versus the "oppositional I"

## Reflection

This externalises the problem of anorexia and creates a clear vision of the central problem  and helps to extract the client from the morass of confused feelings that usually populate the mind of clients with this type of eating disorder. It then becomes clear that the client is fighting the battle to gain control of their physical body and that they have a choice as to who they are going to support in this battle their "I" or the "oppositional I".

### 2. Sandplay sequence for changing the battle/ game plan between the "oppositional I" and the "I."

### Step 1:

- Invite the client to choose pieces that place boundaries around the "oppositional I" to contain its power and cut off its influence upon, and proximity to their body.

### Step 2:

- Invite the client to strengthen their 'I' by choosing pieces that bring extra resources and power to support the "I" in the battle against the oppositional "I".

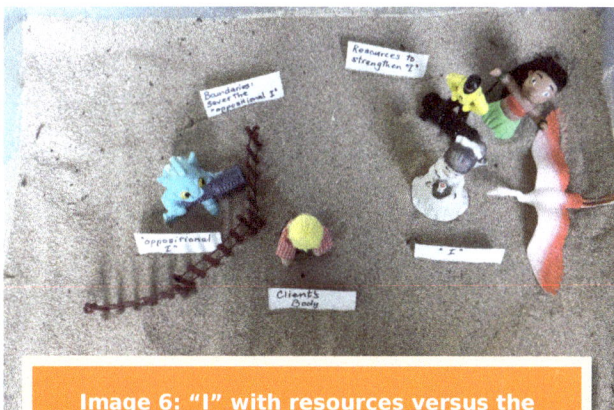

Image 6: "I" with resources versus the "oppositional I" surrounded by boundaries

**Reflections**

This tray is thereafter repeated regularly in following sessions so the client can physically externalise and appraise the battle and view for themselves what resources need to be added to the side of the "I" and what constraints are to be placed around the "Oppositional I". It is generally a very popular sandplay sequence as it gives the client a sense of independent agency over their eating problem, rather than feeling inextricably subject to their anorexia problem.

### 3. Sandplay sequence to strengthen the "I"

**Step 1:**

- Ask the client to select a piece to represent the "I" and place in the centre of the sandtray.

- Invite the client to list all the qualities that when experienced strengthen their "I" and help it win the battle against the "oppositional I". These qualities often include love, praise, self-acceptance, being in nature, warmth, sunshine, compassion, and peace.

**Step 2:**

- The client then selects pieces to represent each one of these qualities and places them around their "I" or integrated self. The client then photographs this sandplay to remind them of the qualities that support and strengthen their resolution to support their bodily health.

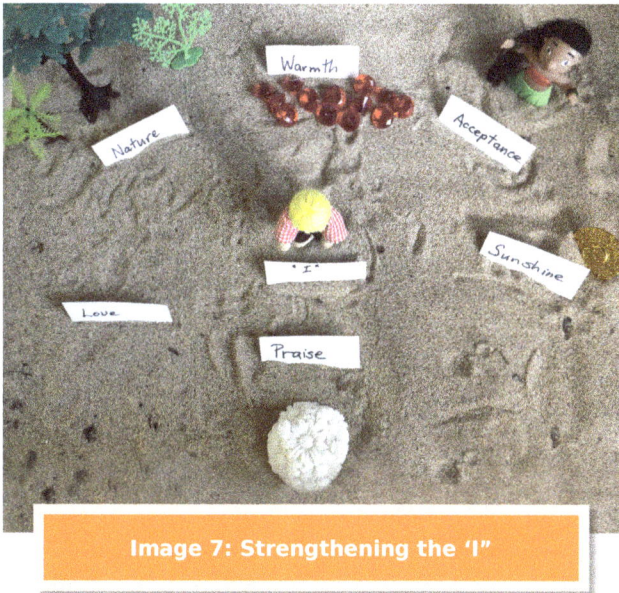

**Image 7: Strengthening the 'I"**

### Reflection:

For each quality listed by the client we consider ways of increasing access to that quality in their lives through behavioural modifications, engaging in new supportive activities, creating new social activities that the client can experience as supportive. Here, I would engage the significant members of the family system in supporting these positive changes in the client's life.

### 4. Sandplay sequence to explore the qualities that feed the "oppositional I"

### Step 1:

- Request the client to choose a piece to represent the "oppositional I" and place this in the sand tray.

- Ask the client to list the emotional triggers that run their eating problem and create labels for each of these emotional triggers.

## Step 2:

- Request the client to select pieces to place in the sandtray that represent each of these triggers.

- Explore these triggers one at a time in depth to uncover the dynamics that drive the eating problem for the client. This sandtray may take more than one session to complete.

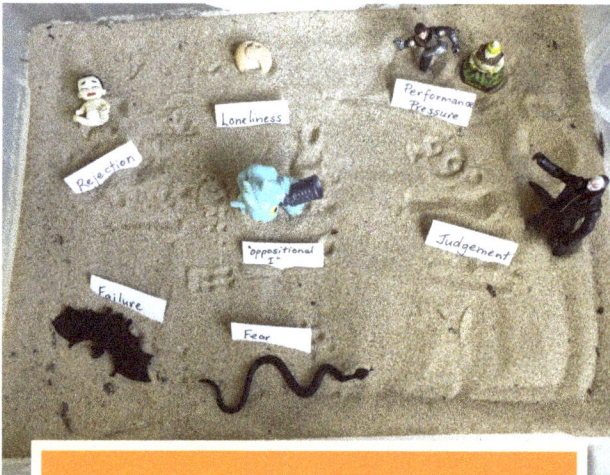

Image 8: Feeding the "oppositional I"

## Reflection:

In reflection we work on each one of these emotional triggers that provide the cognitive affective substructure for the anorexia by using a combination of strategies best suited for the particular client which may include cognitive reframing, psycho-education, behavioural modifications and somatically based interventions. Illustrated below is a typical somatically based intervention drawn from *Holistic Counselling: A New Vision for Mental Health* (Sherwood, 2010) that would be implemented to consolidate the sandplay sequences that have been elucidated above.

**Pre intervention preparation**

1. Select one of the emotions that feed the "oppositional I" and encourage the client to establish a clear intention to release it and replace it with a positive alternative.

2. Assist the client to learn the bodily signs of dissociating and leaving their body and teach them how to remain present in their body (Sherwood, 2010, pp. 136-141)

3. Resource the client by invoking strength through engaging with figurines selected by the client from the sandplay pieces that help them feel empowered in the face of the "oppositional I" that is driving their eating disorder.

**Intervention**

1. Client to recall an incident around a particular quality identified in their sandtray above eg. "failure," when they experienced being controlled by the "oppositional I" and hence began to starve themself by refusing for example, to share a birthday party meal with their friends.

2. Ask the client where in the body they felt most uncomfortable when they remember the incident.

3. Request the client to step into that part of the body and sense how the breath is not moving freely and what shape it makes. Ask the client to step back and draw the shape of the contracted breathing.

4. Ask the client to step into the shape they have drawn with their whole body, so the whole body takes on this shape.

5. Invite the client to share their feelings when they are in this restricted gesture and their earliest memories of feeling like this.

6. Find if the client experiences their feeling as an attack or an abandonment or both.

7.  Apply the appropriate sequences to free the client from this negative experience and restore the flow of breathing (Sherwood, 2010, p.245)

8.  Resource again with the strong positive images selected from the sandtray pieces. The client breathes into their body where the tension is experienced, the healing power of these images. They client is asked to experience these qualities as flowing into their body in colour, form and gesture. The client is encouraged to feel the flow of these positive qualities in their breathing as it moves through their body.

This sequence would be undertaken for every one of the negative triggers that the client identified in the sandplay above, using specific incidents that the client can recall that illustrate how the triggers work in their life.

## 5. Sandplay sequence showing the victorious "I"

Following work to weaken and demobilize the strategies of the "oppositional I" regardless of the model of therapy that you have used to facilitate this transition, the following sandplay is predicated. It is most useful to complete the therapeutic process with a sandplay devoted to the "Victorious "I", the one who has overcome the eating disorder of anorexia. The "victorious I" is now the owner and inhabitor of their body and the "oppositional I" has been confined to distant quarters. Directions to the client are as follows.

**Step 1:**

*   Place in the centre of the sand tray pieces that represent your body and your "I".

*   Select the qualities of strength that now protect your body and your "I" from the "oppositional I" and place them around the centre piece.

**Step 2:**

- Find a piece to represent the "oppositional I" and place in the sandtray.

- Rearrange all pieces so that they reflect where you now stand in relation to this situation.

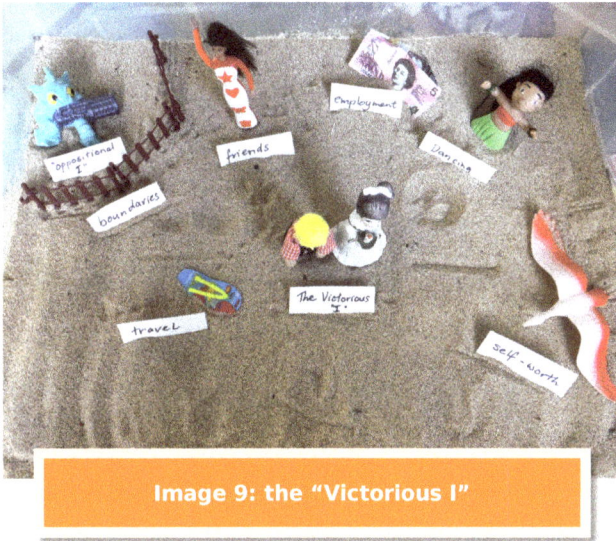

Image 9: the "Victorious I"

**Reflection**

The final arrangement in the sandplay gives an excellent indication of where the client has moved to in overcoming their anorexia. It also is a photograph the therapist can encourage them to keep on their phone and regularly check and appraise on a daily basis to ensure that they are still on track over the following weeks and months.

In essence, working with clients experiencing anorexia can be effective using both undirected and directed sandplay to provide orientation to their problems and to reveal some of the deep dynamics that are keeping them in this destructive cycle. However, it is most often that the directed sandplay sequences are a significant component of therapeutic interventions that work towards promoting insight into the dynamics of anorexia and which offer transformative pathways for the client as they search for, and commit to recovery.

## REFERENCES

Australian Government Department of Health Department (2005) Section 1: *Anorexia Nervosa: the facts* https://www1.health.gov.au/ internet/publications/publishing.nsf/Content/mental-pubs-a-anorex-toc~mental-pubs-a-anorex-1 Accessed 26-12-19.

Bernock, D. (2019) *Emerging With Wings: A True Story of Lies, Pain, And The LOVE that Heals* https://www.goodreads.com/quotes/tag/trauma Accessed 24-12-2019.

Hurst, K (2013) Placing the focus on perfectionism in female adolescent anorexia nervosa: three cases of the use of augmented Maudsley Family Based Treatment. In *Journal of Eating Disorders* 1, (O28) DOI https://doi.org/10.1186/2050-2974-1-S1-O28

Mantilla, E., Norring, C & Birgegard, A. (2019) Self-image and 12-month outcome in females with eating disorders: extending previous findings. In *Journal of Eating Disorders* 7(15). https://doi.org/10.1186/s40337-019-0247-1

Maudsley centre (**www.maudsleyparents.org**). Accessed 15-1-2020.

Selvini Palazzoli, M. (1989) *Family Games: General Models of Psychotic Processes in the Family*

N.Y., Norton and Co.

Selvini Palazzoli, M., (1978) *Self-starvation: From individual to family therapy in the treatment of anorexia nervosa* N.Y., Jason Aronson.

Sherwood, P. (2017) *Creative approaches to CBT*. London: Jessica Kingsley.

Sherwood, P. (2010) *Holistic Counselling: a new vision for mental health.* Bunbury, Sophia Publications.

Waldman, A., Loomes, R., Mountford, V & Tchanturia, K (2013) Attitudinal and perceptual factors in body image distortion: an exploratory study in patients with anorexia nervosa. In *Journal of Eating Disorders* 1(17). https://doi.org/10.1186/2050-2974-1-17

## CHAPTER 3
# Obsessive Compulsive Disorder (OCD)

*Traumatized people are not suffering from a disease in the normal sense of the word- they have become stuck in an aroused state. It is difficult if not impossible to function normally under these circumstances.*

Peter A. Levine (2019)

Obsessive-compulsive disorder (OCD) is a mental health condition characterized by distressing, intense, consuming and intrusive thoughts. This is often accompanied by compulsive and repetitive physical behaviours or irrational mental obsessions. Most well known compulsions include washing hands, cleaning repetitively including clothing and other objects that are already clean, checking repeatedly locks, lights, windows, doors and other objects, hoarding objects and repetitive body movements. Common obsessive mental thoughts include a fear of germs and disease, intrusive sexual thoughts, recurrent fears of violence, death or tragedy to self and or family members and obsessive fears around particular objects, numbers or combinations of numbers. It is defined as problematic and becomes concerning when the behaviour or behaviours prevent or seriously hinder the person from leading a normal life and routinely, regularly and negatively disrupt family relationships and activities. Obsessive compulsive disorder prevents the person who is suffering in this way, from living a healthy personal and social life which should include working and socialising routines, as well as maintaining the normal human activities of washing, showering, cleaning, and eating.

Thus the sufferer is prevented by their time-consuming repetitive rituals and activities, from engaging in a comprehensive social life and satisfying human relationships. OCD becomes a seriously debilitating disorder as it progresses and the sufferer is unable to maintain the normal activities required of a human being. As it becomes severe, the sufferer can only survive if they have convinced other family members to support their behaviours and obsessions in some form. They can only co-exist in a co-dependent relationship with a "carer" or "enabler," or their physical health deteriorates rapidly.

Research reveals that OCD runs in families and can be considered a "familial disorder" in that it is rare to find a child with OCD who does not have at least one parent with similar inclinations or behaviours. The disease may span generations with increased probability that relatives of people with OCD will be more likely to manifest OCD at some point in their lives. It is a condition that can affect people of all races and social backgrounds but there is a higher preponderance among females. The diagnostic criteria for OCD cited by Nichols, (2018) are as follows:

- the presence of obsessions, compulsions or both

- the obsessions and compulsions are time-consuming or cause clinically significant distress or impairment in social, occupational, or other important areas of functioning

- The obsessive-compulsive symptoms are not due to the physiological effects of a substance, for example, drug abuse or medication for another condition.

- the disturbance is not better explained by another mental disorder

Over 2% of Australians are diagnosed with OCD which appears most often in childhood, adolescence or early adulthood (SANE, 2018). This can therefore significantly adversely affect the person's life and their opportunities. Treatments include prescribed drugs, family system therapies, psychodynamic therapies, psycho-education and behavioural therapies.

Very often, the first step involves re-training the family system members to avoid enabling the sufferer by assisting in rituals and complying with orders or requests by the sufferer. This can be very challenging to the whole family system which has become compliant with the OCD sufferer. Accommodating the family routine or lifestyle to meet the OCD needs of the sufferer are significant factors in maintaining the OCD behaviours, as indirectly it gives the sufferer control over the persons in their family system as well as control over the family environment. In some cases, the sufferer may become a tyrant in the family system, preventing members from leaving the house, sleeping in particular rooms, eating in certain ways or at certain times. Reducing and eliminating compliant behaviours by family members is essential in reducing the disorder particularly when it is occurring in children and adolescents (Bipeta, Yerramilli, Pingali, Karredla, & Ali, 2013; Storch et al., 2007). When parents acquiesce to OCD behaviours that are aggressive, manipulative and abusive, they increase the likelihood of the behaviour re-occurring (Storch et al., 2012). Research has shown that if family accommodation and enabling of the client's rituals can be reduced during therapeutic treatment for OCD, then there are significantly better treatment outcomes for the sufferer and the family. (Merlo, Lehmkuhl, Geffken, & Storch, 2007; Storch, Lehmkuhl, et al., 2010).

Prior to commencing therapy with a child or adolescent suffering from OCD, it is recommended that the therapist coaches the parents to develop strategies and skills that provide alternatives to their enabling behaviours and enmeshed conversational responses. These new behaviours and communication patterns include not assisting in the ritual, not accommodating in time or space for it, not engaging in irrational discussions about the ritual, not providing objects or assistance in any way that support the ritual, not becoming angry, distressed or disturbed but instead walking away from the sufferer during the ritual, so they are denied attention or engagement of any sort. This appears in case work to be an essential component for rapid progress of recovery with the child or adult client suffering from OCD.

Prior to commencing the directed sandplay sequences, begin with nondirected, unstructured sandplays in which the client works spontaneously with what arises for them. Once a trusting therapeutic relationship has been established and the client has sufficient strength to face the trauma, the following directed sandtray sequences are implemented in the order in which they are presented below. They may be interspersed with spontaneous sandplays or with other therapeutic strategies determined by the unique needs of the individual client, as the therapeutic process proceeds.

## 1. Sandplay sequence 1: the Voice and its battle to control the physical body

The client must be prepared by previous unstructured, non directive sandplays for this directed sequence which aims to expose them very consciously to the battle that is going on for possession of their body by the OCD Voice.

**Step 1:**

- Invite the client to choose a piece that represents their body and place it in the centre of the tray.

- Ask the client to then choose a piece that represents "the voice" that tells them what to do, how often and when, and place it on the left side of their body.

- Suggest to the client that they choose a piece that represents their spirit, the best of who they can be which I call their "I" or integrated self, and to place it on the right side of their body.

**Step 2:**

- Reflect on the battle between the two forces for the client's body. Consider with the OCD sufferer, the pros and cons of each one of these two figurines and ask the client to identify which is winning the battle and which one the client would like to win the battle.

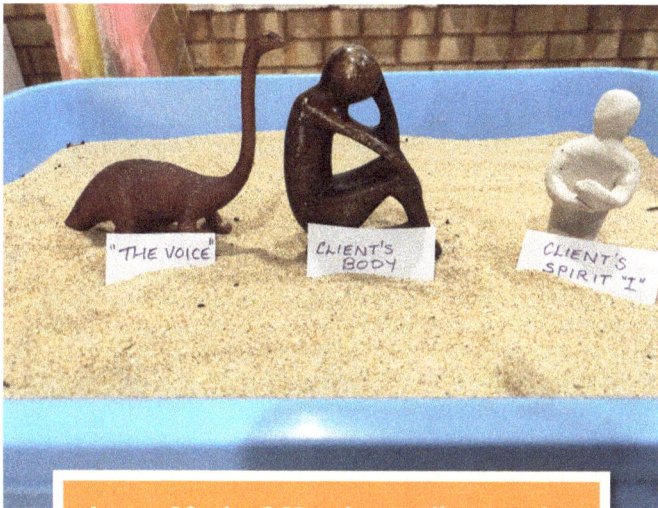
Image 10: the OCD voice vs client's voice

**Reflection:**

By externalising the OCD Voice and separating it from the client's "I", the client's perspective on their problem is changed. Usually, it changes from a feeling of powerlessness and hopelessness to one of hope and higher motivation. This sandplay process offers a unique and powerful way of exposing the game plan and as such empowering the client with a new vision and hopeful possibilities of changing this destructive game plan.

## 2. Sandplay sequence  for uncovering what is behind the voice

Invite the client to continue to explore in more depth the figurines selected in tray one.

### Step 1:

- Invite the client to identify what is inside the OCD Voice that makes it so powerful and choose a piece to represent it. If the client is uncertain, one can suggest that they imagine stepping inside the piece. It is here that the clients are often shocked. They most often recoil and discover most commonly that it is full of cruelty or hatred. They choose a piece to represent this and place it behind the OCD Voice. All pieces are labelled as we move through the sequences so that it is very visible to the client.

### Step 2:

- Ask the client to choose a piece or pieces that represents what is inside their body. Most commonly this is a feeling of emptiness, hollowness, powerlessness, fear and /or anxiety. This piece is placed behind the body.

### Step 3:

- Suggest the client now choose a piece to represent what feelings are inside of them when they reflect upon the previous pieces. Without hesitation, most clients invariably reply fear of something that they can often identify such as dying, losing my family or being killed.

Image 11: what is behind the OCD voice and defeated "I"

## Reflection:

Together with the client reflect upon the sandplay and ask some directive questions during this process which include:

What is the "deal" between the OCD voice and your spirit/self? The answer is usually: "if I do what it tells me I will be protected against my fears of..." This leads to the question: "What is the connection between cruelty and the OCD Voice"? The answer from the client is usually that the cruelty is attached to the OCD Voice but it is hiding behind it, and it enjoys living off the client's energy and suffering or some similar comment. This then usually leads to a frank appraisal of the cost of having the OCD Voice and its attachment running the client's body versus the client's own spirit or integrated self.

The problem then therapeutically is that the client will not cut off the OCD Voice unless they have a better way of dealing with their fears. Then proceed to add the pieces which represent the resources that are required for the client to feel that they would be able to cease listening to the OCD Voice. This is illustrated in the sandplay sequence below.

### 3. Sandplay sequence for protecting the fearful one

**Step 1:**

Invite the client to create a wall between their body, their spirit/ self and the OCD Voice and monster attached to it. Clients may make this themselves, from wood, clay, or a selection of objects from the tray. It is clear in this sandtray, that the client is not confident that the OCD Voice can be contained, as it still has its head between the fencing pickets.

**Step 2:**

Ask the client to select pieces that represent how they would need to feel in their body and in themself in order to be able to cut off the OCD Voice and its attachment.

Ask the client to place the symbol between their body and its hollow feeling. In this case the client chose peace to be placed between their body and their feeling of emptiness and hollowness.

Ask the client to choose another positive quality and to place it between their self and the negative feelings of fear. In this example protection was chosen and placed in the sandtray there to counter their fears.

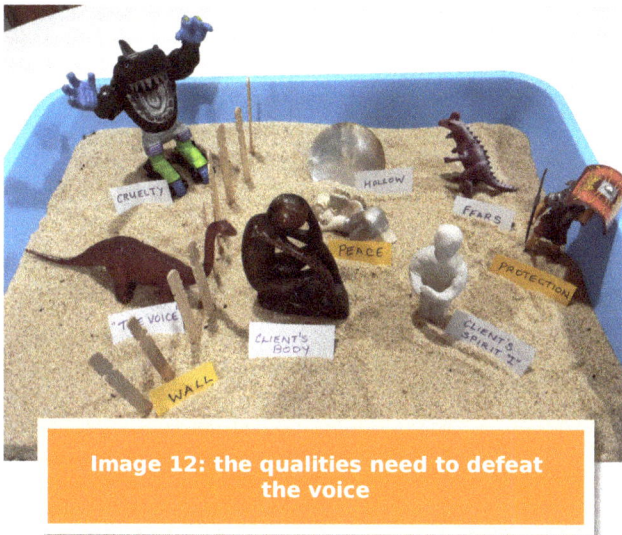

**Image 12: the qualities need to defeat the voice**

## Reflection

### Therapeutic issues

By this stage, following the completed tray above, the therapeutic issues are clear. Firstly, this then involves working with the client's fears in order to manage, reduce or eliminate them. Usually by the time a client has OCD, there are a considerable number of core fears and at the deeper level of exploration, one usually finds at least eight to ten traumatic incidents from childhood that need to be addressed. The second therapeutic task is to disempower, reduce and eliminate the OCD Voice and its attachment. Of course this leads to the third and primary therapeutic task which is to create a "protector" that is positive and skilful prior to removing the OCD Voice.

In therapy it is unlikely that the client is willing to eliminate dysfunctional protectors against fear unless they have a better option. These days with the absence of culturally protective figures and rituals, the task is left to the therapist. Human beings have always been, and still are, prone to fear whenever they experience life-threatening or disturbing situations. Therefore the creation of a protective archetype or image that the client can identify with and learn to use as a protective figure is essential to counter the OCD Voice and its attachment. The positive archetype strengthens the client's spirit/ self to stand strongly on their own ground in the world and direct their own lives. In essence, OCD is a primitive attempt by a person in fear and terror to survive by using a negative life-destroying archetype, the OCD Voice and its attachment which I term the "oppositional I". It is important that one does not commence therapeutic tasks 1 or 2 until this clear positive archetype has been established. How the therapist processes the above issues that have surfaced in the sandplay depends on their particular modality of training.

## Therapeutic interventions

### *Resourcing the positive archetype*

I will briefly outline the therapeutic interventions I use as a somatically based holistic counsellor. The first task would be to find a powerful, positive archetype from the human symbolic or spiritual world that the client feels a connection with strongly and whom they feel could protect them against what they experience as fear. Then by a process of using the bodily senses namely, breathing, gesturing, sounding the name of the archetype and drawing, painting or making the archetype's gesture in clay, the client comes to embody the protective power of the archetype (Sherwood, 2010, pp97-103). If the flow of the positive archetype's gesture is not fully in the breathing and gesture of the client, then it will not prove an adequate resource in the face of the trauma that must be released.

### Transforming the fears that provide the scaffolding for the OCD behaviours

1. Make a list of the OCD behaviours that the client wants to stop. Select to work on one at a time using a specific incident from the client's experience attached to each of the OCD behaviours.

2. Teach the client to stay in her/his body and not leave by becoming aware of their consciousness in their body. Assist the client to learn the difference between being present in their body through grounding and what is meant by dissociation. Also teach them skills on how to remain present. Educate the client to note the signs of dissociating and how to return by stamping feet and becoming present (Sherwood, 2008, p.78).

3. Invoke the positive archetype through the eleven (or seven) directions sequence developed by Sherwood, (2008 p.107 2013, p.109).

4. Remind the client that she/he is not the "OCD voice" and that they have power over it.

5. Complete a somatic process called enter-exit behold by which the client steps into the part of the body where the tension is experienced when they recall an incident of being controlled by the OCD voice. They then draw the shape of the tension and then step into the contracted breathing shape with their whole body (Sherwood, 2013, p94.) The gesture will reveal the underlying incident of fear upon which the current OCD behaviour is scaffolded.

6. Once this incident is established the therapist needs to work with the client to remove attacking forces and to resource with positive qualities the one who has been abandoned or attacked. The precise steps for these processes are outlined in Sherwood (2013, pp 80-83).

### Removing "OCD Voice"

1. Remove the OCD Voice by cutting the cord and the attachment of cruelty which is afflicting the client. Once the client has identified where the "OCD Voice" is located, then there is a focal point upon which to focus. This is done actively, using sound, gesture and imagery. Begin with a cutting sound of "kkk" or "ch ch ch "or "t t t " or "c t  c t ". Then the client is encouraged to burn off the entire "OCD Voice" and attachment using fire sounds "fssh" "fsshh" until the client can visualize it turning into ash. Then blow the ash away with a wind sound "whosssh, whoosh", and associated gesture.

2. Replace the place of the OCD Voice with the positive protective archetype and a boundary, using a positive, protective earth sound such as "d,d,d,d" or a vowel sound, whatever the client likes and experiences as positive and protective.

3. The above exercise should be completed at the end of every session when working on the client's fears and whenever the client hears the OCD Voice. In addition, for the next three weeks the client must practice resourcing daily with the positive archetype so that the positive protective archetype becomes embodied in their breathing, thinking and visualising to such a degree that the client can invoke the positive archetype at will and with ease.

Detailed sequences for dealing with Voices, including the OCD Voice are outlined in Sherwood, (2013, pp.110-111).

## 4. Sandplay sequence for reinforcing the power of the protective positive archetype.

During the above therapeutic work, it is recommended that the therapist uses the following sandplay sequence at the beginning and sometimes the end of the sessions which are involved with transforming their fears. The therapist can direct the client to make a sandtray showing the power of their protective archetypes to keep them safe and to allay their fears. They need to place the protective archetype and sometimes additional protectors, as in the case illustrated below, to protect themselves from their fears. Such a sandplay is illustrated below. The archetype chosen here is a wise and powerful American Indian chief. There are solders maintaining a protective boundary around the client as well. It is always worth getting the client to photograph this sandplay and use it to resource themselves for at least the next seven days.

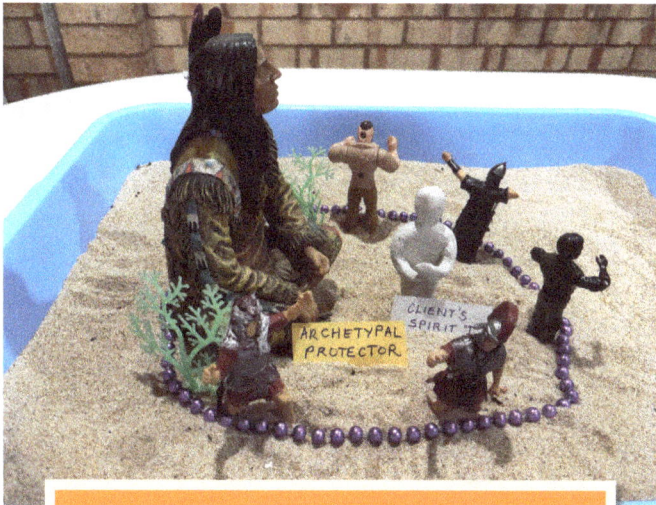

Image 13: the powerful positive archetype defeats the voice and protects the client

## REFLECTIONS

OCD, especially when it is a habit that has been established over years, is a challenging and difficult phenomenon to work with in therapy. However, observations reveal that directed sandplay sequences are invaluable in making explicit the dynamics of the problem so that the client has greater perception and more penetrating insight into their problem. This gives the client increased confidence and a greater capacity to heal from the disorder. The deep psychological dynamics of OCD is so forgotten by the client, so unknown to their conscious mind, that sandtray is an ideal medium for bringing it back to consciousness. Only then can the fragmented experiences which shatter the healthy self be re-integrated into the self, producing greater psychological health and freedom from the tyranny of OCD.

As Branden (2019) so poignantly and accurately indicates, "The greater a child's terror, and the earlier it is experienced, the harder it becomes to develop a strong and healthy sense of self." It is the gift of sandplay both directed and undirected, to provide a safe contained medium to facilitate the client's movement from fear and terror to self-awareness and empowerment. Sandplay can become a medium through which the client may discover the dynamic which includes their own strength to take control of the lives with a more integrated and functional sense of self.

## REFERENCES

Bipeta R., Yerramilli S. S., Pingali S., Karredla A. R., & Ali M. O. (2013). A cross-sectional study of insight and family accommodation in paediatric obsessive-compulsive disorder. *Child and Adolescent Psychiatry and Mental Health,* 7(1), 1–11. Doi:10.1186/1753-2000-7-20

Branden, N (2019) *Six Pillars of Self-Esteem* https://www.goodreads.com/quotes/tag/trauma Accessed 24-12-2019.

Johnco, C., (2016) Managing Family Accommodation of OCD in the Context of Adolescent Treatment Refusal: A Case Example. In *Journal of Clinical Psychology* 72(11) 1129-1138.

Published online 2016 Sep 18. doi: 10.1002/jclp.22393

Levine, P (2019) https://www.goodreads.com/quotes/tag/trauma Accessed 24-12-2019.

Merlo L. J., Lehmkuhl H. D., Geffken G. R., & Storch E. A. (2009). Decreased family accommodation associated with improved therapy outcome in pediatric obsessive-compulsive disorder. *Journal of Consulting and Clinical Psychology,* 77(2), 355–360. doi:10.1037/a0012652

Nichols, H (2018) *What is obsessive compulsive disorder?* https://www.medicalnewstoday.com/articles/178508.php

SANE, (2018) **https://www.sane.org/information-stories/facts-and-guides/obsessive-compulsive-disorder.**

Sherwood, P. (2017) *Creative approaches to CBT.* London: Jessica Kingsley.

Sherwood, P. (2010) *Holistic Counselling: a new vision for mental health.* Bunbury, Sophia Publications.

Sherwood, P. (2008) *Emotional Literacy: the heart of classroom management.* Melbourne: ACER.

Sherwood, P. (2013) *Emotional Literacy for Adolescent Mental Health.* Melbourne: ACER.

Storch E. A., Geffken G. R., Merlo L. J., Jacob M. L., Murphy T. K., Goodman W. K. ... Grabill K. (2007). Family accommodation in pediatric obsessive-compulsive disorder. *Journal of Clinical Child & Adolescent Psychology,* 36(2), 207–216. doi:10.1080/15374410701277929

Storch E. A., Jones A. M., Lack C. W., Ale C. M., Sulkowski M. L., Lewin A. B. ...Murphy T. K. (2012). Rage attacks in pediatric obsessive-compulsive disorder: Phenomenology and clinical correlates. *Journal of the American Academy of Child & Adolescent Psychiatry,* 51(6), 582–592. doi:http://dx.doi.org/10.1016/j.jaac.2012.02.016

Storch E. A., Lehmkuhl H. D., Ricketts E., Geffken G. R., Marien W., & Murphy T. K. (2010). An open trial of intensive family based cognitive-behavioral therapy in youth with obsessive-compulsive disorder who are medication partial responders or nonresponders. *Journal of Clinical Child & Adolescent Psychology*, 39(2), 260–268. doi:10.1080/15374410903532676 [

 Waldman, A., Loomes, R., Mountford, V & Tchanturia, K (2013) Attitudinal and perceptual factors in body image distortion: an exploratory study in patients with anorexia nervosa. In *Journal of Eating Disorders* 1(17). https://doi.org/10.1186/2050-2974-1-17.

# CHAPTER 4
# Traumatic Mutism

*"The conflict between the will to deny horrible events and the will to proclaim them aloud is the central dialectic of psychological trauma."*

Herman, Judith (2019)

C onsiderable attention has been given to selective mutism, a condition characterized primarily by extreme anxiety in certain social situations which render the person, often a child, unable to speak, although they are able to speak and do speak fluently at home or when they are with people with whom they feel comfortable and relaxed. Shipon-Blum (2019) cites the characteristics of selective mutism as defined by the DSM IV (2000) as:

1. Consistent failure to speak in specific social situations (in which there is an expectation for speaking, e.g., at school) despite speaking in other situations.

2. The disturbance interferes with educational or occupational achievement or with social communication.

3. The duration of the disturbance is at least one month (not limited to the first month of school).

4. The failure to speak is not due to a lack of knowledge of, or comfort with, the spoken language required in the social situation.

5. The disturbance is not better accounted for by a Communication Disorder (e.g., stuttering) and does not occur exclusively during a Pervasive Developmental Disorder, Schizophrenia, or other Psychotic Disorder.

These characteristics have been confirmed by the DSM-5 (Newman Mercardo, 2019). Of these selectively mute children, 90 % also have a social phobia or anxiety disorder co-occurring (Shipon-Blum (2019). Selective Mutism is most likely to emerge in childhood and according to research appears to result from the complex interplay of genetic, developmental, environmental and temperamental factors ( Hua and Major, 2016).

Much has been written about selective mutism while the traumatic mutism is given little attention. There appears to be little evidence that selective mutism is primarily related to trauma whereas traumatic mutism is always connected with one or more traumatic experiences. It is characterised by the suddenly ceasing to speak in all situations and all settings including home, school, with close friends and family, following an experience that the client perceives as traumatic (Shipon-Blum, 2019). It occurs across the age spectrum and may emerge in childhood, adolescence or adulthood. In my experience, once the traumatic event is integrated into the client's experience, they resume speaking in all environments. In many cases, the refusal to speak has some anxiety in its substructure, but it is primarily driven strongly by protective factors of rejection and punishment towards the perceived aggressor who is, in their view, the cause of their traumatic experience. There is also a sense of hopelessness and powerlessness in relation to the perceived aggressor. Refusing to speak to anyone not just distresses the perceived aggressor but more importantly gives the client their only sense of power in a situation in which they otherwise feel entirely powerless. In this chapter, the focus will be only upon traumatic mutism of this type as outlined above, and directed sandplays that have enabled such clients to work through their trauma and commence speaking again across the spectrum of persons in their lives. Commonly clients in the category of traumatic mutism have been ten years of age or older and more commonly older teenagers and adults.

## Sandplay sequences

Before commencing directed sandplay sequences, it is recommended that the client does a few nondirective sandplays first so the therapist can understand better the client's experience of their mutism and to develop an empathetic therapeutic relationship with the client. Such clients often become profoundly engaged in sandplay as the pressure or expectation that they will speak is entirely removed. They therefore experience a safe environment with no speaking performance pressures, so are more likely to relax. It gives them the opportunity to express themselves wordlessly. Over the period of a few sandplays, they begin to communicate with me through signs or writing notes which are not forms of communication they have used frequently prior to commencing sandplay. At this point one can begin to introduce directed sandplays.

### 1. Sandplay sequence on the fearful versus hostile non speaking self.

**Step 1:**

- Ask the client to choose a piece to represent the person who threatens you and place it in the sandtray.
- Invite the client to select a piece that represents themself and place it in the sandtray.

**Step 2:**

- Suggest the client select a figurine that represents their feelings of fear when they face the threatening person and place this behind the figure of themselves.

**Step 3:**

- Ask the client to choose a figure that represents the one who is angry towards the threatening person and wants to punish them and also place this figurine in the sandtray near themself.

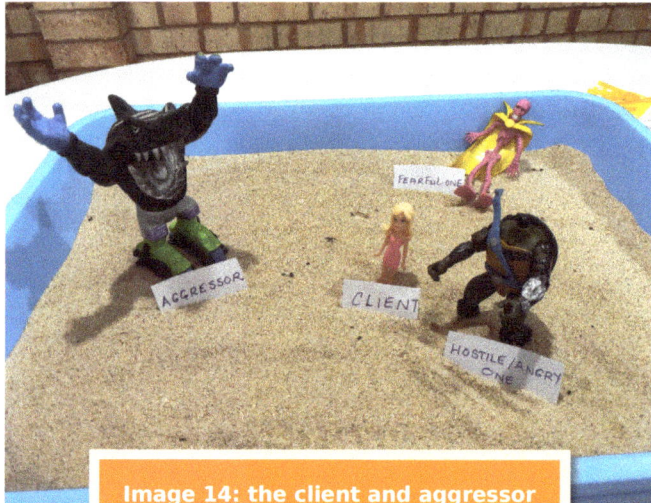

Image 14: the client and aggressor

## Reflection:

At this time the therapist can reflect in words upon the dilemma the client is facing and point out that they are caught between the fearful one who just wants to hide, and the hostile one who is trying to protect the client from the perceived aggressor. I observe the client's body language and facial expressions closely to ascertain if my reflections are accurate. On occasions, the reflections will motivate the client, especially if an adult or older teenager to write about their experiences with the perceived aggressor. Often it is as though a secret has been released and some will even begin to speak about the aggressor and the feelings of resentment towards them.

## 2. Sandplay sequence to build protection for client in face of aggressor

**Step 1:**

- Ask the client to take the pieces of the fearful one, the client and the aggressor and place in a new separate sandtray.

- Invite the client to choose figurines that could protect the fearful one from the aggressor and place around the fearful one.

**Step 2:**

- Invite the client to place boundaries around the aggressor and continue to build them until they feel safe and protected from the perceived aggressor.

- Suggest the client find a figurine that represents them feeling safe and protected and place it beside their original figurine in the sandtray.

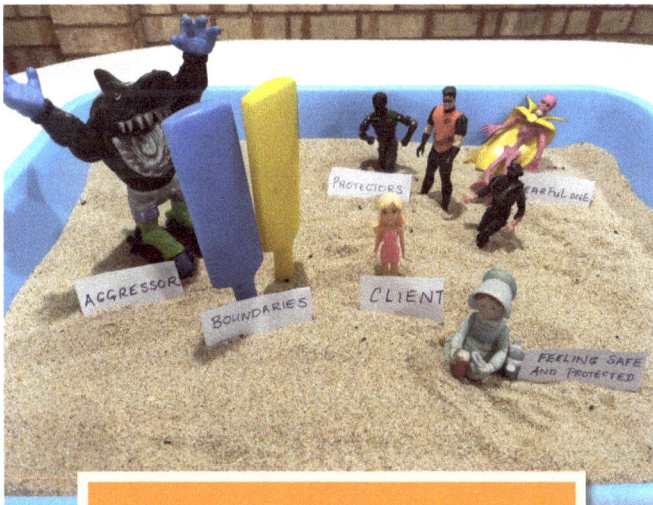

**Image 15: building protection in face of aggressor**

**Reflection:**

Reflect on the sandtray by suggesting to the client positive ways of feeling safe and protected in their life that have more advantages than disappearing into fear and hostility and the associated mutism. This can be done as a white board exercise or in conversation.

Here the therapist would also intervene with somatically based sequences drawn from holistic counselling to deal with the specific incident which has triggered the client into mutism by asking them to write it down. The sequences would involve an empowerment sequence to remove the force of the attacker which the client has experienced as so overwhelming that they have withdrawn into the untouchable and unreachable space of non-speaking or silence (Sherwood, 2010, pp141-144). It is essential that this step is completed using whatever modality the therapist finds effective.

### 3. Sandplay sequence  to transform the hostile self into the speaking up self

**Step 1:**

- Invite the client to select figurines that represent the aggressor, themself and the hostile one and place in tray.

- Encourage the client to act out upon the aggressor through gesture, their hostile feelings of what they would like to do to the perceived aggressor such as slap, hit, shake or squash them

**Step 2:**

- Suggest that the client explore alternative ways of dealing with the aggressor such as clear boundaries, speaking up for their rights and bringing protective figures with them to confront the aggressor. Invite the client to select figurines to represent these options.

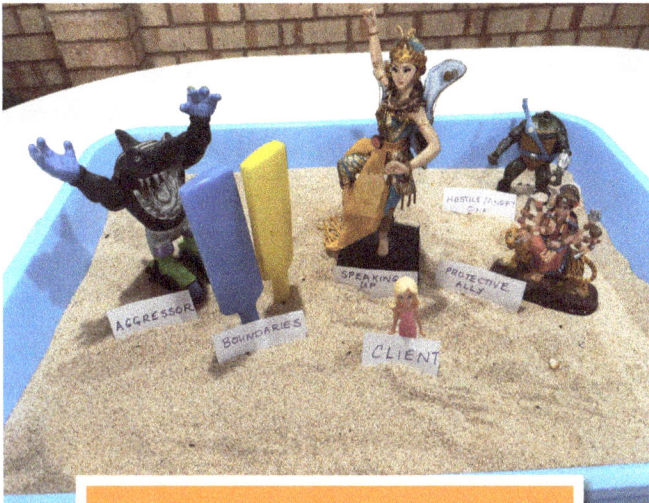

Image 16: the client supported by a positive archetype

## Reflection

The therapist would consider the advantages of these positive ways of managing the perceived aggressor and in particular work with the client to establish clear bodily boundaries using a protective dome made of the single syllable "d,d,d,d" which is repeated everyday out loud and internally in silence, in the presence of the perceived aggressor. For details of this effective embodied boundary process see Sherwood, (2017, p.77).

## 4. Sandplay sequence of forgiveness towards the aggressor

### Step 1:

- Ask the client to place figurines of themself and the perceived aggressor in the sandtray.

- Invite the client to choose a figurine that could forgive the aggressor (even if they cannot at this moment in time) and place between themself and the aggressor.

- Ask the client to find another figurine that represents someone who could forgive the aggressor.

- Repeat this a third time.

- Suggest that the client breathe in the forgiveness from each of these figurine symbols into their body where they feel the tension, when they reflect upon the aggressor and themselves.

**Step 2 :**

- Ask the client to select a figurine that could forgive themself for their anger and hostility towards the perceived aggressor and place in the sand tray.

- Breathe in this energy of self-forgiveness represented by the figurine they have chosen.

- Invite the client to re-arrange the sandtray or remove or add pieces as they observe this tray of figures of forgiveness, so as to make it exactly as they would like it.

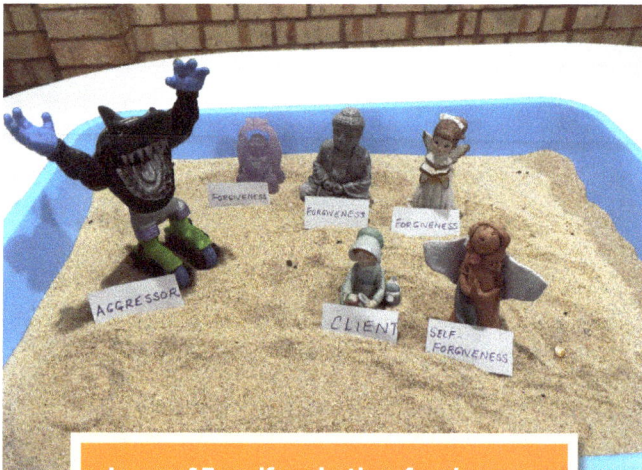

Image 17: self and other forgiveness

**Reflection**

This is usually a profound sequence in which the client starts to breathe differently and sometimes shows signs of being deeply moved such as shedding tears or remaining transfixed on the sand tray in deep reflective thought. This tray is photographed for the client to reflect upon and to continue to breathe in forgiveness for the aggressor and self.

## 5. Sandplay sequence of speaking up

**Step 1:**

- Invite the client to select pieces for the self, and the one they have forgiven (the perceived aggressor) and place in the sandtray.

- Ask the client to place a protector figurine next to them and between them and the perceived aggressor.

- Suggest the client place a figurine representing forgiveness and place next to themself.

**Step 2:**

- Invite the client to represent speaking up for their needs and their truth to the perceived aggressor and choose a symbol to represent this act.

- Encourage the client to speak up or write down what they wish to say and place it between themselves and the perceived aggressor.

- Invite the client to rearrange the sandplay once they have spoken up either verbally or in writing so that it reflects how they now feel.

Image 18: speaking up

## Reflection

This series of sandplays with clients suffering from traumatic mutism has often been effective in clinical work and resulted in the client actually speaking up to the perceived aggressor. Many times it has resolved the issue that originally traumatised them with the aggressor. The sandtray is particularly suited to working with clients suffering from traumatic mutism as it provides a wonderful, rich and varied nonverbal world for the client to explore. This facilitates the client's expression of their unresolved traumas, and provides the opportunities for them to integrate their traumatic experience in a non verbal way so that they are freed to move on and speak up for their needs and rights. Finally, it provides a place for the client's perspective and a space to freely and unrestrainedly express their experience. This is a process that can give a voice to the unspeakable, give power to their powerlessness, and words to their repressed pain and hostility. It can then provide a gateway for healing and transformation, and a bridge back into the social world where they have re-established a place to stand. They have then reclaimed the right to speak up for what they need.

## REFERENCES

Herman, Judith (2019) *Trauma and Recovery: The Aftermath of Violence - From Domestic Abuse to Political Terror* https://www.goodreads.com/quotes/tag/trauma. Accessed 24-12-2019.

Newman-Mercardo, S (2019) *The selective mutism foundations influence over selective mutism in the diagnostic and statistical manual of mental disorders* . www.selectivemutismfoundation.org  Accessed 30/12/2019.

Hua, Alexandra; Major, Nili  (2016) Selective Mutism. In *Current Opinion in Pediatrics:* February 2016 - Volume 28 - Issue 1 - p 114–120

doi: 10.1097/MOP.0000000000000300

Sherwood, P. (2017) *CBT and artistic therapies: an unlikely marriage.* Bunbury: Sophia Publications.

Sherwood, P. (2010) *Holistic counselling: A New Vision for Mental Health.* Bunbury; Sophia Publications.

Shipon-Blum E (2019) *Selective Mutism – A Comprehensive Overview*

https://selectivemutismcenter.org/whatisselectivemutism/ Accessed 29-12-19.

# CHAPTER 5

# Body Dysmorphic Disorder (BDD)

*"It is an awful thing to be betrayed by your body. And it's lonely,
because you feel you can't talk about it. You feel it's something
between you and the body. You feel it's a battle you will never win . . .
and yet you fight it day after day, and it wears you down.
Even if you try to ignore it, the energy it takes to ignore it will exhaust you."*

David Levithan (2019)

B ody dysmorphic disorder was first documented by Morselli in 1886 who coined the word from the Greek, meaning "ugly face". He described it as a "subjective sensation of deformity or physical defect that causes the patient's belief of being noted by the others, although the physical aspect appears normal" (cited in Fiori, P., & Gianetti, L., 2009). Body Dysmorphic Disorder (BDD) is characterised by obsessional, distorted thinking about one's appearance believing that one's visage in particular is deeply marred, scarred, distorted, contorted in some profoundly ugly and unredeemable way, despite the evidence  that one has a normal appearance. The dysmorphia may also include other body parts such as hands, arms, legs, genitalia, body shape and body size. These distorted beliefs run the client's life so that most of their day is spent focused on these thoughts and they often also become obsessive about mirrors either regularly checking themselves or completely concealing all mirrors. As a result of this cognitive distortion accompanied by deluded feelings of self-hatred, self-rejection and self-repulsion, the sufferer may withdraw from work and social life because they believe that others perceive them the same way that they perceive themselves. In some extreme cases, the pain of the "perceived ugliness" and self-annihilation may be so great that it leads to suicide (Phillips, 2004).

This delusional pre-occupation with a particular bodily part or feature as grossly ugly is projected onto people around them who they often perceive as staring at them, talking about them or mocking them in some way so that their social life and social activities become fraught with anguish and suffering. Often the sufferer will become more and more socially isolated in an attempt to avoid the deluded but perceived pain of daily rejection by other people (Phillips, 1993). In reality, the perceived flaw is either entirely unnoticeable by people or non-remarkable. Rather the sufferer is trapped in a world in which they perform repetitive, meaningless, purposeless movements, tasks, gestures or actions to try to manage the defect and control their appearance which may take from three to eight hours a day, depending upon the severity of the condition (Phillips, 2004). Common obsessional behaviours include mirror checking, excessive grooming, repeated hair styling, unnecessary skin treatments, unnecessary surgical procedures, skin picking, unnecessary dietary restrictions, and excessive exercising. Such repetitive and pointless activities will consume inordinate amounts of the sufferer's time and are constantly on the mind of the person afflicted with body dysmorphia. Despite repeated questioning of friends, relatives and close associates about their appearance, the sufferer rejects all reassurance or confirmation by these significant others, that they are of normal appearance and have nothing to be concerned about (Victorian State Government, 2019).

Some research suggests that body dysmorphia dominates males, others females, while yet other research suggests that it is evenly spread across genders. However, there is general agreement that it most commonly starts during adolescence (Albertini and Phillips, 1999). Gundstad and Phillips (2003) note that body dysmorphia is commonly associated with depression, with over 58% of sufferers identified as depressed. In addition to depression, other common co-morbid behaviours include addictions, social phobia, obsessive compulsive disorder (OCD), and personality disorders. All these are common among sufferers of body dysmorphia. Approximately 2% of the population are afflicted with body dysmorphia (Victorian State Government 2019.)

At the psychological level, body dysmorphia emerges as a psychological experience of perceived or actual rejection. Usually the sufferer was triggered into the disorder after rejection by a significant person in their lives perhaps a lover, a parent or an intimate person. The rejection is totally indigestible in terms of rational analysis, so the sufferer seeks to externalize it, albeit in a distorted way, to avoid in some contorted way the pain of the rejection. The sufferer attaches this loss to a physical feature that they believe must have caused the rejection. Pre-occupation with this bodily feature acts as a defence mechanism against future social relationships and a block to any future wounding from rejection. Winograd (2019) describes this dynamic lucidly:

> Body dysmorphic disorder wedges itself between the sufferer's desperation to connect and the fear that they might be rejected while attempting to do so. This serves the purpose of preventing rejection; if one is constantly dismissing oneself it becomes much more difficult to be rejected by another human being. For many highly sensitive body dysmorphic disorder patients, rejection is experienced as the ultimate proof that something must be inherently defective about them. For this to be the case is often interpreted as absolute confirmation that they can never be loved. Taking the risk of possible rejection might

mean experiencing these dire consequences, and to most, the benefits do not out-weigh the consequences. Thus body dysmorphic disorder exists in the space of the relational ambivalence, completely changing the focus from fears of intimacy and fundamental feelings of inadequacy to excessive attention towards perceptible physical features.

Clients suffering from body dysmorphia have lower self-esteem than that of an equivalent control group and in addition suffer from self-ambivalence. They are re-evaluating their self worth by the second, the minute, the hour, and the day so that their self-judgment and ambivalence is intensified in a downward spiral (Labuschagne, cited in Moulding et al 2016). They avoid dealing with the fears of rejection and inadequacy of the self by believing, albeit falsely, that if they somehow looked different, all of their feelings of inadequacy, ugliness, defectiveness and unlovability would fade away. This pattern has often been inherited from a parent, probably a mother whose pre-occupation with physical appearance has indirectly or directly enabled the sufferer as a child, to develop an artificially strong connection between physical appearance, lovability and social acceptance. Winograd (2019) powerfully summarises how a person's deepest shame becomes associated with a bodily feature and this connection is consolidated cognitively many thousands of times a day to determine the entire of a person's self worth:

> Within the construct of body dysmorphic disorder, a body part takes on an identity of its own. The body area of concern becomes profoundly associated with the individual's sense of self. The individual with BDD misses the forest through the trees, and rather than seeing many different body parts that together shape outward appearance, the despised physical feature becomes the

focal point of their existence. It can easily become the singular element within the person's life and a gauge that determines the entirety of their self-worth.

Therapeutically body dysmorphia is difficult to process and many clients afflicted by it have been in therapy for years with only very marginal benefits. The sandplay sequence used below however, has resulted in major changes and shifts towards healthy body imaging in many clients suffering from body dysmorphia.

## 1. Sandplay sequence showing the battle for the body between the self and the anti-self

### Sandplay sequences

As with the previous issues, it is necessary for the therapist to make a diagnostic appraisal of the level of trauma and the appropriate timing of the following directed sandplay interventions. Usually before commencing directed sandplay sequences, the therapist will invite the client to complete some nondirective sandplay, so that they familiarize themselves with the technique of sandplay. It also provides the therapist with the opportunity to develop an empathetic therapeutic relationship with the client.

### Step 1:

- Ask the client to choose a piece that represents the critical voice that is continually belittling and criticising their body. The size of the piece chosen reflects the level of power that the client experiences that this voice has over their life.

- Invite the client to select a piece that represents their self, the best of who they can be. The size of this piece represents the power they experience in relation to their positive self.

**Step 2:**

- Suggest the client select a figurine that represents their body and place it between the critical voice which we call the anti-self and the piece that represents their self.

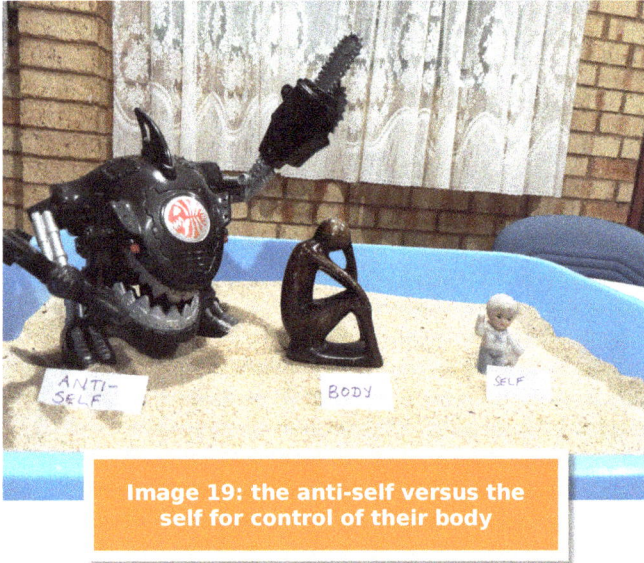

Image 19: the anti-self versus the self for control of their body

**Reflection:**

Clearly identify that this is a battle for their body between their self, and the anti-self. Ask the client to consider why the anti-self has become so huge and this leads to the frequency of thoughts that feed it and a range of cognitive restructuring activities to move thinking away from the anti-self and towards the self. The therapist should here reflect with the client, on why the self is so small and why there is a lack of support for it. Note the lack of energy devoted to its growth and lack of focus upon the self and its positive attributes. The battle between the anti-self and the self is clearly identified as the goal of therapy which is to disempower the anti-self because it is costing the client their life, their work, friends, love, happiness and the good things in life. The concurrent goal is to empower and revitalise the self which can bring the client friends, happiness, a social and work life. This can only be achieved when it is freed from the oppression of the anti-self. Ask the client, as long as they have reached the age of ten years or more, to write down a clear list of how they want to feel differently in their life, or the behaviours that they want to change in their life. Work from the client's wish list for change as the therapy proceeds through different sessions. In this case of body dysmorphia, the client's wishes are usually around not being dominated in their mind and actions by this figure called the anti-self, and being freed from particular specific situations and triggers that the client has listed as troublesome. Each situation becomes the focus for a session if required.

## 2. Sandplay sequence to understand the weapons of the anti-self used in the battle against the self to win possession of the client's body

### Step 1:

- Ask the client to place in the sandtray figurines representing the anti-self or critical voice and their body.

- Invite the client to choose a figurine that represents their self, the one that is afflicted by the negative critical voices of the anti-self that is constantly belittling and shaming their body or parts thereof.

### Step 2:

- Invite the client to write down all the negative feelings that the anti-self directs towards the self. In this example there are three of these negative feelings representative of the types of negative feelings that clients' express: namely self-loathing, self-annihilation and self criticism.

- Suggest the client find figurines that represent each of these attacks upon the self by the anti-self and have them place these pieces in the tray in relation to the self.

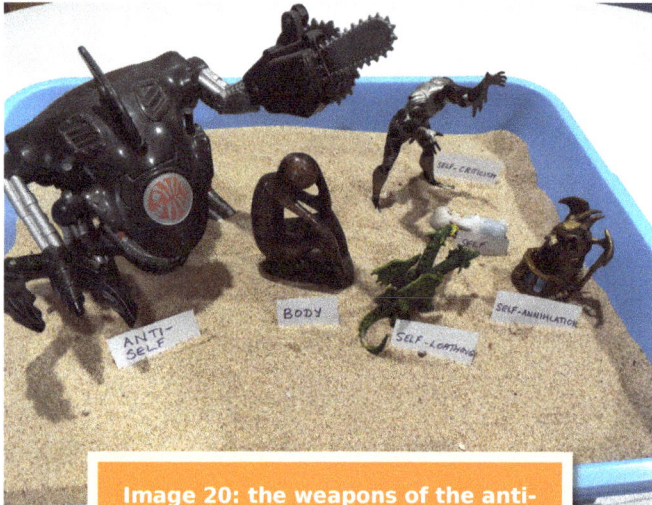

Image 20: the weapons of the anti-self against the self.

## Reflection

Reflect on the sandtray with the client by asking the client to identify clearly why the self is losing the battle and why the anti-self is winning. At this point, ask the client to write down the negative messages that the self has internalised as a result of being defeated in this battle with the anti-self for their body. A classic list will include:

"I am ugly"

"I am a failure"

"I am useless"

"I am unlovable"

"I am stupid"

Essentially, in working therapeutically with clients suffering from body dysmorphia, one reveals a mountain of body shame that has been internalised since early childhood and has essentially led them to create a distorted cognitive affective link between their "unworthy" body and all their feelings of failure in their world. The self is diminutive and has been entirely obliterated by the focus on the physicality of the body. The body is seen as the centre of their emotional universe instead of the self.

At this point, it is beneficial if the client completes a number of somatically based interventions to go to the origins of these negative messages about their body and to release and transform them into positive messages. The basic technique used to effect this transformation in somatically based holistic counselling is termed the EEB or enter-exit-behold. This technique developed by Tagar, and modified by Sherwood, is detailed in Sherwood (2017, pp104-107 and 2018, pp 100-102.)

1. Recall a specific incident where you experienced the anti-self giving you the message that "I am ugly". Where in your body do you experience the unease or tension when you recall the incident and the negative message?

2. A scarf is placed on the floor in front of the client. The side closest to the client is the present moment and the side furthest away the original experience which is running the negative message.

3. Place a cushion in the area furthest away and label it "the ugly one".

4. The client is then asked to place their hands on the part of the body where they feel the negative message and then to step over the scarf and then to imagine that they are stepping into that part of their body. They are then asked to sense the shape of the tension in the body.

5. This is followed by the client stepping backwards over the scarf and drawing a picture of the shape of the tension.

6. Place a picture on the cushion of the shape of the tension.

7. The client is then asked to step into the shape with their whole body as if they were fitting themselves into the contracted shape they have drawn. They identify any feelings that come up when their body is in that shape.

8. The client is then asked if they can then sense the earliest memory of their body being in that shape.

9. This is followed by asking the client: "Did you experience feeling that you were attacked or abandoned?" Then suggest to the client that they step backwards into the safe space and shake off any residue of the experience.

10. The client should be resourced with positive qualities if they experienced being abandoned or rejected. Here use a sand tray so that the client can choose a figurine to represent the three year old, or whatever age they experienced themself to be when they completed the enter-exit-behold sequence detailed above. Request that the client place a figurine, for example, representing the three year old in the sandtray. Here the client surrounds their figurine self with the qualities they needed but did not receive at the time. These might be figurines representing acceptance, love, warmth, nurturing, care or any others that the client identifies. It is vital that they then experience breathing these qualities that are represented by the figurines they have selected, into their body, and particularly to the "wounded one" to bring about their recovery and healing.

If the client also experiences being attacked either verbally or physically particularly through criticism and judgment then an empowerment sequence developed by Tagar and cited in Sherwood (2010) is required and it is briefly outline as follows:

1. Ensure the client is present and grounded in their body and that they have positive archetypal resources, that is, figurines representing inner strength and courage, before commencing this sequence.

2. The client steps back into the shape of the tension they have drawn. They then sense outwards as to how they feel the criticism, judgment or physical force is attacking them. The client is asked: "Is it like a punching, kicking, stabbing, poking, twisting, wringing, suffocating?" Then direct the client to step out of the gesture and make the shape of the force they experienced attacking them upon the cushion.

3. As they repeatedly stab, hit, poke, kick, whack, twist or otherwise repeat the force on the cushion, facilitate the client to find a sound for the force that represents the shape of the force they experience as attacking them.

4. The therapist makes the sound at the client standing a distance away and the client pushes it away with a loud earth sound such as a "d" or "g". This is done gradually as the client's resistance to the sound is initially poor. Eventually immunity is built up and the client's body no longer reacts to that sound. Then the client feels empowered and free from the attacking force at last. (Sherwood, 2010, pp 141-144).

This is followed up by strengthening the client's boundaries with a protective dome as follows:

1. Ask the client to stand in their new position of strength. Request them to build a protective dome all the way around themself as they make the repetitive sound 'd d d' to keep all attacking forces out.

2. The client is directed to imagine they are building a protective dome made out of a material of their choice such as bullet proof glass, steel, bricks, gold, fire or diamonds.

3. They must repeat this dome daily for three months gesturing it while speaking the sounds out loud. Whenever they hear the voice of the anti-self they repeat this boundary silently.

4. Clients are encouraged to take this image with them and, whenever the voice of the anti-self arises to cut it off using the sound 'kkk' and to burn it into ashes using the sound "sshh" or similar sounds. For details of this effective embodied boundary process see Sherwood, (2017, p.77).

This somatic work is completed following sandtray sequence two and alongside sandtray sequence three below. It is repeated for all the core negative messages such as "I am ugly, a failure, useless, unlovable" that the client has listed.

### 3. Sandplay sequence to empower the self and place boundaries against the anti-self controlling their body and their life.

**Step 1:**

- Invite the client to select figurines that represent their self and their body and place them in the sandtray.

- Invite the client to list all the positive messages that are now part of the cognitive framework of the self, having completed the somatic sequences above namely: "I am attractive, I am a success, I am lovable" and "I am useful" as in this example.

- Select figurines that represent these positive messages and place then around the self.

**Step 2:**

- Now select a figurine to represent the anti-self and place in the sandtray with a significant boundary around it.

**Image 21: the self winning the battle for the body by overcoming the anti-self.**

## Reflection

At this stage, invite the client to make a daily practice of placing a boundary between their body and the anti-self. Also at this point in the therapeutic process, the client usually notes that the negative anti-self voices focused on the body are beginning to diminish and the positive self appraisal is enlarging and strengthening in their lives. Here work with the client to re- establish positive bodily experiences of their self-worth that embrace social, educational and/ or work opportunities.

## 4. Sandplay sequence of the empowered self winning the battle for the body

### Step 1:

- Ask the client to place figurines of themselves, and their body in the sandtray.

- Invite the client to choose figurines that represent the new cognitive affective messages that the empowered self is now capable of manifesting, which include in this example: "I am lovable, I am useful, I am attractive and I am a success."

**Step 2:**

- Ask the client to select a figurine that now represents the anti-self and place in the sand tray

- Invite the client to re-arrange the sandtray or remove or add pieces as they now observe and experience the dynamic between the body, the self and the anti-self.

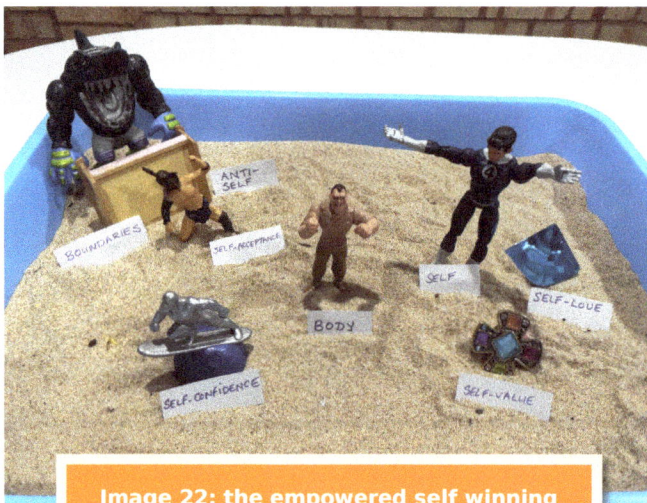

Image 22: the empowered self winning the battle for the body

**Reflection**

This is usually a profound sequence in which the client starts to breathe differently and sometimes shows signs of being deeply moved such as reflecting quietly on the sand tray in deep reflective thought. This tray is photographed for the client to continue to reflect upon.

Usually by the time this sand tray is reached the anti-self has now considerably diminished in size and on some occasions has been eliminated from the tray entirely. The piece representing the self has enlarged considerably and the piece representing the body is now usually upright and strong and has a powerful rather than oppressed position in the sandtray.

Body dysmorphia therapeutically reveals the significance of messages given to the child from the family system and other significant adults about their body as shameful and not attractive or good enough. This is the result of an impoverished world view that focuses upon material realities rather than the complex dimensions of a human being. Especially absent is the core parental task of nurturing and building positive self-esteem. Van M. Derber (2019) accurately notes the impact of such emotional toxicity on the body:

> All emotions, even those that are suppressed and unexpressed, have physical effects. Unexpressed emotions tend to stay in the body like small ticking time bombs— they are illnesses in incubation.

So, for the child, whose body or appearance is frequently belittled by parents or significant adults or where the family currency is physical appearance, then that ticking time bomb is likely to surface during the vulnerable years of adolescence or early adulthood.

## REFERENCES

Albertini RS, Phillips KA. 33 cases of body dysmorphic disorder in children and adolescents. *Journal of the American Academy of Child and Adolescent Psychiatry*. 1999; 38:453–459.

Fiori, P., & Gianetti, L., (2009) Body dysmorphic disorder: a complex and polymorphic affection. In *Neuropsychiatric Disease and Treatment*

*Journal.* 2009: 5: 477-481  doi: 10.2147/ndts6744

Gunstad J, Phillips K.A. Axis I co-morbidity in body dysmorphic disorder. *Compr Psychiatry.* 2003; 44(4):270–276.

Levithan, D (2019) *Everyday*  https://www.goodreads.com/quotes/tag/dysmorphia. Accessed 31-12-2019.

Moulding, R., Mancuso, S. Rehm, I., Nedejkovic, M., (2016) The self in obsessive compulsive related disorders, hoarding disorders, body dysmorphic disorder, and trichotillomania. In Kyrios, M., Moulding, R., Doron, S., Bahr, S., and Nedejkovic, M. *The self in understanding and treating psychological disorders* pp112-133.  (Cambridge: Cambridge University press)

Phillips, K., (2004) Body dysmorphic disorder: recognizing and treating imagined ugliness. World Psychiatry, Feb; 3(1): 12-17.  PMC1414653  https://www.ncbi.nlm.nih.gov/pmc/articles/PMC1414653/   Accessed 31-12-2019.

Phillips KA, McElroy SL, Keck PE, Jr, et al. Body dysmorphic disorder: 30 cases of imagined ugliness. American Journal of Psychiatry. 1993;150:302–308.

Phillips K.A, & Castle D.J., (2002) Body Dysmorphic Disorder. In: Castle D.J., Phillips K.A, editors. *Disorders of Body Image.* Hampshire: Wrightson Biomedical; 2002. pp. 101–120.

Sherwood, P. (2017) *CBT and artistic therapies: an unlikely marriage.* Bunbury: Sophia Publications.

Sherwood, P (2018) *Creative approaches to CBT* London; Jessica Kingsley.

Sherwood, P. (2010) *Holistic Counselling: a new vision for mental health.* Bunbury, Sophia Publications.

Van M. Derbur, Marilyn (2019) *Miss America by Day* https://www.goodreads.com/quotes/tag/trauma Accessed 24-12-2019.

Victorian State Government: Better Health Channel (2019) *Body dysmorphic disorder* https://www.betterhealth.vic.gov.au/health/conditionsandtreatments/body-dysmorphic-disorder-bdd  Accessed 31-12-2019.

Winograd Arie M, (2019) *Face to Face with Body Dysmorphic Disorder: Psychotherapy and Clinical Insights*

https://www.goodreads.com/quotes/tag/body-dysmorphic-disorder Accessed 31-12-2019.

# CHAPTER 6
# Addiction

*"There are all kinds of addicts, I guess. We all have pain. And we all look for ways to make the pain go away."*

Sherman Alexie (2019)

In relation to substance intake, drug addiction can be defined as the loss of control over drug intake and the compulsion to take drugs to the detriment of one's health, one's intimacy, one's work and one's social life. This includes both prescribed and non prescribed drugs as well as socially approved recreational drugs such as smoking and drinking alcohol. Drug ingestion results in changes in the brain that often alter both the brain functioning and structure, and create a basic drug addiction circuitry that is molecular, neurochemical and/ or neuroanatomical. Ingesting the drug creates pathways which reward the user with feel good chemicals. (Koob, 1996). Addiction occurs when the person needs more and more of the substance to obtain the same rewarding emotions and eventually they need more and more of the substance to avoid the painful symptoms of withdrawal even if there are no longer many rewarding emotions. The repeated use of drugs eventually impairs the brain functioning, particularly in areas relating to insight, self-control, stress management, executive decision making, consequential thinking and problem solving and this further weaken the person's capacity to resist the addictive process (National Institute on Drug Abuse, 2018).

The prevalence of particular types of addictions varies in different countries and cultures and Australia's profile is highest in relation to alcohol. The 2016 National Drug Strategy Household Survey report shows that:

> the decline in daily smoking slowed in 2016 but improvements were seen among people living in the lowest socio-economic area; certain groups disproportionately experience drug-related risks and recent use of illicit drugs was particularly high for people who identified as homosexual or bisexual; just under 4 in 10 Australians either smoked daily, drank alcohol in ways that put them at risk of harm or used an illicit drug in the previous 12 months. (AIHW, 2017).

In addition, 17% of Australians drink alcohol at level that makes them at risk for alcohol related diseases, 26% consume alcohol monthly, that places them at risk of harm and 35% of drug addiction cases requiring medical intervention relate to alcohol (AIHW, 2017).

Drug addiction is usually a result of an attempt to alter emotion and mood, and or to be part of a social group. Risk factors have been identified as trauma history, poverty, familial drug use and violence, failure at school or work, prolonged unemployment, and associated aggressive or problem behaviours. Protective factors include a warm loving relationship with at least one significant person, a sense of belonging to a group or community, successful achievements at school or work, religious or spiritual connectedness, experiencing a purposeful connection to life through engaging in activities relating to family or community. An emerging phenomenon in Western post-industrial societies has been the search for meaning and the avoidance of boredom. Campbell (2001, p.165) cited in Sherwood (2010) observes that in his clinical work with heroin users the most common comments are like: "If I don't use drugs, I will be bored. I started using because I was bored". The failure of society with the demise of the institutionalised religion to provide some meaning and purpose in human existence, is endemic to the problem of youth drifting aimlessly and seeking some experience that will give them purpose. Dunselman (1993, p.15) in his classic work, *In Place of Self*, clearly enumerates the connection between drug addiction and the failure of the person to find a pleasurable, purposeful and meaningful place for their self in their world without drugs. He quotes an opium drug addict:

> The first time is a dream, an unbelievable experience of paradise, an encounter with the gods. The first few times are beautiful so you are reconciled to your existence. You are able to forgive, and at last you can breathe deeply and freely again.... it's not long until the day comes when a triple dose no longer has any effect. Even if you shoot up twice in quick succession, there's hardly any effect. Everything is reversed. It's only when you don't take anything that you notice anything – all the pain and misery there is in the world. From that moment you pay a high price to feel normal. You suffer merely to avoid suffering.

There are many models of addiction recovery in relation to alcohol addiction which Miller and Hester (2003, p.8) summarise. These include the moral model based on legal sanctions and self-control; the spiritual model based upon restoring faith in the spiritual world through groups such as Alcoholics Anonymous; the educational model which resorts to providing knowledge; the social learning model which focuses on skills training; the biological model which focuses on hereditary counselling; and the conditioning model which focuses on operant conditioning; the family systems model which focuses upon family therapy; the harm minimisation model which focuses on reducing the hazards of addiction and a range of other counselling modalities.

Sandplay therapy for clients suffering from addiction and trauma is relatively new and Freedle's et al (2015) research is landmark. In a multi-intervention program including sandplay over 16 weeks the outcome was promising. Participants reported significantly improved daily functioning at home, school, and community and reduced the severity of their substance abuse. In addition, it was noted that they exhibited reduced symptoms of distress associated with their trauma exposure. Both the participants and an independent evaluator concluded that the sandplay was the most critically useful intervention during the therapeutic program. Marcelo Merlini (2004) cites the use of it in public hospital work with drug addicts. As part of a multi intervention approach, sandplay therapy was used for drug addiction recovery. In addition to the sandplay sequences below, it is essential to engage the client in family therapy, community support groups appropriate to the client's interest and in acute cases where detox is necessitated then it is recommended that clients commence in a therapeutic residential community.

## 1. Sandplay sequence for revealing the core dynamic of the thoughts directing addiction

When working with clients suffering from addiction, begin with undirected spontaneous sandplays to see what emerges from the client's experience and work to build a therapeutic relationship that is nonjudgmental but has clear boundaries. It is highly recommended to not see clients who are under the influence of any drugs. Establish a contract in the first session with the client in relation to this condition of therapy. In session one, it is advised to work to facilitate the client obtaining support from other services as required. It is important that the client establish a clear list of the therapeutic goals, that is, the changes in their thinking, feeling and behaviour that they wish to achieve through therapy. This is critical as too often clients come to therapy with addictions and are only presenting in therapy as a result of family pressure. It is helpful to ensure that the clients are engaged in the process of recovery before commencing. Begin with the following trauma informed directed sandplay to enable the client to better understand what is driving their addiction at the most external level, "the craving".

**Step1:**

- Invite the client to select a piece that represents their physical body and place it in the centre of the sandtray.

- Ask the client to reflect on the state of their physical body. Why have they chosen this particular figurine to represent their physical body? In addiction case work, this piece often reveals bodily depletion and exhaustion.

**Step 2:**

- Invite the client to choose a piece that represents their human spirit, the best of whom they can potentially be, which represents their highest and most creative potential. Name this piece as their "I" or highest self potential and ask the client to label it as such, and place the piece on the right of the piece representing their body. Then reflect with the client on their vision of who they could be without the addiction, their highest potential as a human being. Here it is critical that they build a highly motivational vision of health, growth and taking back control of their life.

**Step 3:**

- Ask the client to select a piece that represents "the craving creature" that tells them that they must have the drug and which will not be satisfied until they have taken the drug. Direct them to place it on the left side of the piece representing their physical body. It is "the craving creature" that tells them that they need the drug in order to be happy, ok or just to cope with their lives and survive. Reflectively converse with the client about the tricks, lies and deceit that the "craving creature" leads them to believe, and in the detrimental activities that it often encourages the client to participate. Note how often these false promises of happiness, cause the client to face great personal cost to their happiness, to their health and wellbeing and to alienate their friends and family.

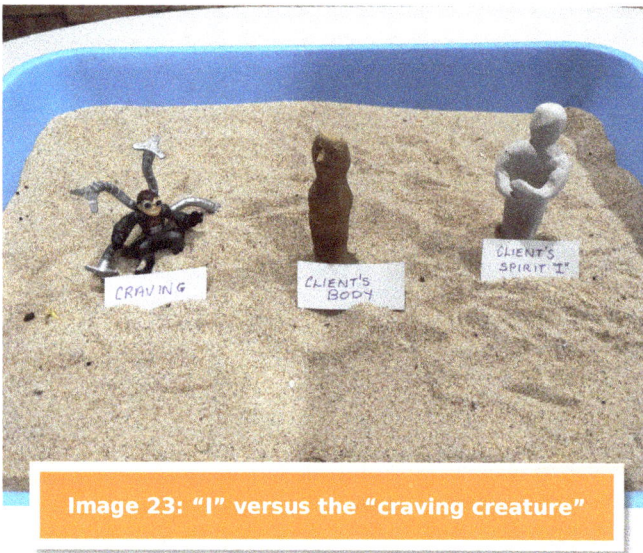

Image 23: "I" versus the "craving creature"

## Step 4:

- Invite the client to step inside "the craving creature" and ask them to select a piece that represents what is inside this "craving" creature and add this to the sand tray as represented below. This piece usually represents the controlling energy of the addiction which is using 'craving" to take control of the client's body and therefore their life.

**Image 24: "I" versus the "craving creature" run by the "oppositional I"**

## Reflection

This starts to elucidate the problem of the addiction relationship and the client begins to gain insight into the dynamic. Ask the client the following question: "Is your primary relationship in life with this being that controls your body and your life through the craving creature?" Their response is usually a definitive "yes." It is this "oppositional I" that steals, lies, deceives, betrays and engages in any sort of behaviour that will obtain the drug during the times that the "craving creature" is used to control the client's body and indirectly through the client's body, the client's thoughts and feelings. It is suggested to the client that this one be named the "oppositional I" because there is a battle for control of the client's body between it and the client's spirit or "I". It then becomes clear that the client is fighting the battle to gain control of their physical body and that they have a choice as to who they are going to support in this battle "their "I" or the "oppositional I" who runs the craving creature, and who lies, is corrupt, manipulative and who offers shady deals.

## 2. Sandplay sequence for revealing the battle/ game plan between the "oppositional I" and the "I."

This sandtray is focused on facilitating the client to explore "the deal" with their "oppositional I," the one who controls the craving and their self. The deal varies depending upon the drug involved. Different drugs have different deals attached to them. In analysis of many clients' experience in completing these sandtrays, particular deals emerge for particular drugs. In the following sandplay, the client is working with alcohol addiction. The deal is always centred around providing relief from grief and loss, loneliness and/or rejection.

**Step 1:**

- Invite the client to choose pieces that reveal the deal between their self and the "oppositional I" to contain its power and cut off its influence upon, and proximity to the client's body. In this case the "oppositional I" is offering an alternative to loneliness and bad memories.

**Step 2:**

- Invite the client to choose pieces that represent "good things "that the "oppositional I" is offering through the deal. The alcoholic "oppositional I" usually offers fun and /or friends but in a superficial way that is escapist, lacks depth and is not enduring past the time it takes to ingest and digest the alcohol. The therapist reiterates that there is a war going on between the "I" and the "oppositional I" for control of the client's body which is the centre piece in the tray. Encourage the client to reflect on this war for control of their body through the craving creature and to become very aware of what it is costing them to surrender to the craving creature.

Image 25: the deal with the "oppositional I"

## Reflections

Through completing this sandplay, the client can physically externalise and appraise the battle and view for themselves what the craving deal offers them through the "oppositional I". It is a generally a powerful sandplay sequence as it gives the client a sense of independent agency over their addiction rather than feeling inextricably subject to their addictive issues.

## 3. Sandplay sequence to strengthen the "I" by meeting its unmet needs.

### Step 1:

- Ask the client to select a piece to represent the "I" and place in the centre of the sandtray.

- Invite the client to list all the qualities that when experienced strengthen their "I" and help it win the battle against the "oppositional I". These qualities often include love, self-acceptance, meaningful work, friends, spiritual / meaningful connections with life, and peace.

## Step 2:

- The client then selects pieces to represent each one of these qualities and places them around the "I" or self. The client photographs this sandplay in order to remind themself of the qualities that support and strengthen their resolution to strengthen their "I".

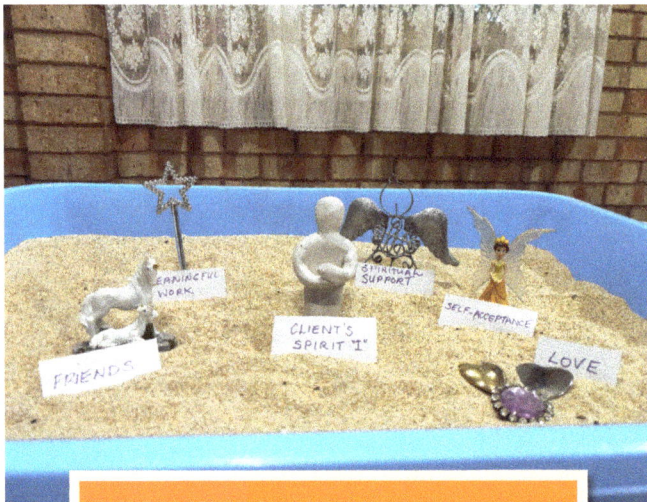

Image 26: Strengthening the 'I' with the missing qualities

## Reflection:

For each quality listed by the client always consider with them ways of increasing access to that quality in their lives through behavioural modifications, engaging in new supportive activities, and through creating new social activities that the client experiences as supportive. Here, if possible engage the significant members of the family system in supporting the positive changes when they are willing and available.

**Reflection:**

The client now works on each one of these missing qualities, the absence of which create black holes in the client's psyche and body that have currently been filled by the drug addiction. At this point, interventions are required over a number of sessions with the therapist using the techniques in which they have been trained which best suit a particular client whether cognitive reframing, psycho-education, behavioural modifications and/or somatically based interventions. Cognitive reframing within the model of somatically based interventions drawn from *Holistic Counselling: a New Vision for Mental Health* (Sherwood, 2010) and *Emotional Literacy for Adolescent Mental Health* (2013) is recommended for holistic somatic counsellors trained in this model. It is essential that each one of the missing qualities which give substance to the client's "I" or integrated self are explored and developed through in depth psychotherapeutic work. In addition, there are all the unresolved traumatic experiences that also run the addiction process which need to be released and transformed. This includes restoring breath back into that part of the body where the client senses emptiness. It is not sufficient just to complete the sandplay elucidated above, unless the therapist has the intention and opportunity of completing many sandplays with the said client, in addition to the ones prescribed herein.

**Pre session intervention preparation**

1. Assist the client to learn the bodily signs of dissociating and leaving their body and teach them how to remain present in their body (Sherwood, 2010, pp. 136-141)

2. Resource by invoking strength giving images selected by the client from the sandplay pieces that help them feel empowered in the face of the "oppositional I" or thought that drives their addiction.

3. Have the client list moments of "craving" when they were overtaken by the "oppositional I" at the expense of friends, family, work, social relationships, etc.

4. Ask the client to write down their positive intentions not to be driven by the "craving creature" in each of the incidents listed in three. Have the client itemise their importance as this will structure the ensuing sessions. Particularly in addiction, it is essential that the therapist works with the client motivation and stated intentions to facilitate the recovery process.

## Enter-Exit-behold somatic interventions for addictions

For each moment identified by the client above, in which the craving over takes the client the therapist requests that they complete the following sequences (Sherwood, 2013, p.94):

**Step 1:**
**Removing the craving creature and the "oppositional I"**

1. Client to recall incident in detail when they were controlled by the craving creature.

2. Ask the client where in the body they felt most uncomfortable when they remember the incident and the craving.

3. Request that the client step over the line marked on the ground by a scarf and imagine stepping into that part of the body where they sense and feel uncomfortable, and sense how the breath is moving in that part of their body. Ask the client: "What is the shape of the tension that is stored there? Is it like a knot, a rock, a ball of string, a lump of concrete?"

4. Have the client step backwards over the scarf and draw the shape of the tension on a piece of paper and place the drawing on a cushion that is on the side of the scarf most distant from themself.

5.  Ask if the client can sense any cords that are attached to the shape. If so, invite the client to draw the cord and to follow literally the cord to the end by imagining walking along the cord. Then ask: "What is at the end of the cord"? Invite the client to draw what is at the end. This is the "craving creature" and behind it they will usually sense the voice of the "oppositional I". This experience reinforces what they have done in the preceding sandplays.

6.  Ask the client: "Do you want to block/cut off the "craving creature" if we can find something strong and positive to accompany you in difficult times, instead of this craving creature?"

7.  Assist the client to find a strong positive archetype. Examples are: Jesus, Nelson Mandela, Buddha, Archangel Michael, Ra, Mother Teresa, Gandhi, or any image that the client relates to that is positive, strong and protective for the client.

8.  Facilitate the client to resource strength using the archetypes by suggesting that the client breathes in the quality of the archetype into their body, speaks its name out loud, and gestures with their body the shape of the power of the archetype. Embody the strength by encouraging the client to walk around the room becoming the gesture of the archetype. Then invite the client to draw the flow of the colour of the archetype's energy coming through their breathing and gesture. This technique is termed "invoking" (Sherwood, 2010, p.97).

9.  Remove the craving creature by cutting the cord with "k k k" or "ch ch ch "or "t t t "or "ct ct". The cord then is burnt off using fire with a sound like "fssh" "sshh" and the craving being reduced to ashes.

10. Resource the client again with the strong positive archetypes.

11. For the next three weeks the client must practice resourcing daily with the positive archetypes so the body has firmly entrenched archetypes that may be invoked at will. Whenever the craving

voice returns the client is encouraged to remember the protective archetype including their sound, their gesture, their colour, and cut off the voice's cord with "kkk" or "ch ch ch" or "t t t" or "c t c t " or "k k k" or any other cutting sound that the client chooses. The cord and the craving being are then burnt off using fire:  "fssh" "fsshh" until it is reduced to ashes.

## Step 2:
## Resourcing the unmet needs that fuel the addiction, that were identified in sandplay 3.

1.  The client selects one of the identified qualities that they require to heal such as warm love.

2.  They sense where in their body they feel the emptiness or hollowness when they think of the absence of this quality in their life and which they are trying to obtain by taking the addictive drug.

3.  They then choose a resource: a person, animal, archetype or natural place that they experience as having an abundance of this quality.

4.  The client then imagines receiving this quality in abundance as they breathe it in to that part of their body. Request that the client give it a colour to keep visualising it flowing through their body to the required hollow place. The client continues doing this until they experience the hollow as filled with the missing quality.

5.  The client then gestures the missing quality and walks around the room in the gesture of the new found quality. They may choose a sound or song that represents the quality and make the gesture or listen to the song.

6.  They then draw the flow of the energy of the quality of warm love moving through their body.

7. The client needs to repeat the above steps for each missing quality that they have named. This needs to be done in the counselling session and in their own lives daily for at least seven days.

**Step 3:**
**transforming the traumatic imprints that drive the need for the addictive substance.**

1. Invite the client to recall an incident around the craving creature driving their behaviour and their feeling of compulsion to take the addictive substance. The client has previously established a strong intention to overcome the craving and to transform in their life.

2. Ask the client where in the body they felt most uncomfortable and tense when they remember the incident in detail.

3. Request that the client steps into that part of the body and over the scarf in an enter-exit-behold sequence and ask them to sense how the breath is not moving freely and what shape it makes. The client then draws the shape of the contracted breathing.

4. Ask the client to step into the shape they have drawn with their whole body, so the whole body takes on this shape.

5. Invite the client to share their feelings when they are in this restricted gesture. Some clients will also recall their earliest memories of feeling restricted in their breathing in this example. This will invoke an earlier traumatic incident which is the foundational trauma behind their addiction.

6. Ask if the client experiences the trauma as an attack or abandonment or both.

7. Apply the appropriate sequences to free the client from this negative experience and restore the flow of breath again (Sherwood, 2010, p.245).

8. Resource again with the strong positive images. Request that the client breathe the positive image into the body where the tension was experienced. The healing power of these images is experienced as flowing into the body in colour, form and gesture.

9. Again encourage the client to cut off the craving creature and the attached "oppositional I" with a loud "k,k," and burn it up with a fire sound like "sshhh" until the client experiences them as reduced to ashes.

This process is repeated for all the moments of craving that the client wishes to transform into healthy decision making so that they are able to free themselves from the control of the "oppositional I". This will take several sessions as each major trigger incident of craving must be addressed and usually there are approximately seven to ten or more sessions.

### 4. Sandplay sequence showing the Victorious "I"

Following the above therapeutic work to weaken and demobilize the strategies of the "oppositional I", it is useful to complete the therapeutic process with a sandplay devoted to the Victorious "I", the one who has overcome the "craving creature" that drives the addiction. The Victorious "I" is now the owner and inhabitor of their body, and the "oppositional I" has been confined to distant quarters or preferably reduced to ashes. Directions to the client are as follows.

**Step 1:**

Invite the client to place in the centre of the sand tray pieces that represent their body and their "I".

Suggest that they now select the qualities of strength that now protect their body and their "I" from the "oppositional I" and place around the centre piece.

**Step 2:**

Suggest that the client find a piece to represent the "oppositional I" and ask them to place it in the sandtray.

Request the client to re-arrange all the figurines so they reflect where the client now stands in relation to the addiction dynamic.

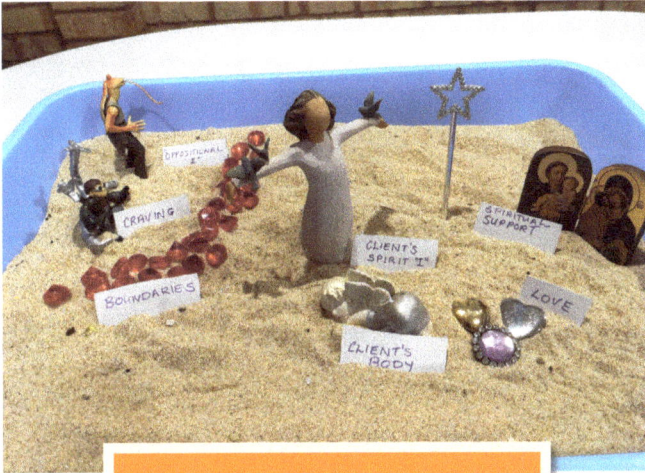

**Image 27: the Victorious "I"**

**Reflection**

The final arrangement in the sandtray gives an excellent indication of where the client has moved to in overcoming their addiction problems. It also important for them to take a photograph of the sandtray of the victorious "I" that they can keep on their phone and regularly check to ensure that they are still on track, over the following weeks and months. If the craving reappears later over a particular incident, then it is indicative that the client needs to return to therapy as soon as possible, so as to transform the experience from the craving that supports the "oppositional I", into a healing place that supports their "I" and their own control over their own life.

Working with clients experiencing problems of addiction can be effective using both undirected and directed sandplay to provide orientation to their problems and to reveal some of the deep dynamics that are keeping them in this destructive cycle where their life is governed by craving rather than by skilful decisions, that support their own and their family interests. These directed sandplay sequences are very powerful in promoting insight and transformation for clients who are suffering from problems relating to addiction.

## REFERENCES

AIHW (2017) *National drug strategy household survey 2016* https://www.aihw.gov.au/reports-data/behaviours-risk-factors/illicit-use-of-drugs/reports Accessed 2-1-2020.

Dunselman, R (1993) *In Place of Self: How drugs work.* Stroud: Hawthorn Press.

Freedle, L., Altschul, D., Freedle, A. (2015) The role of sandplay therapy in the treatment of adolescents and young adults with co-occurring substance use disorders and trauma. In *Journal of sandplay therapy.* 24(2), pp 127-145.

Koob, G (1996) *Drug Addiction: The Yin and Yang of Hedonic Homeostasis* Neuron, 16, 893-896.

Marcello Merlino (2004) Images of time: new departures at a public drug addiction clinic. In Zoja, E., *Sandplay therapy; treatment of psychopathologies* . Daimon Velag, Berlin.

Miller and Hester (2003) *Handbook on Alcoholism treatment approaches: effective alternatives.* Boston: Allyn and Bacon.

National Institute on Drug Abuse (2018) *Drugs, Brains and Behaviour: the science of addiction.* https://www.drugabuse.gov/publications/drugs-brains-behavior-science-addiction/drug-misuse-addiction. Accessed 24-1-2020.

Sherman A, (2019) *The Absolutely True Diary of a Part-Time Indian* https://www.goodreads.com/quotes/tag/trauma. Accessed 24-12-2019.

Sherwood, P. (2010) Search *for yourself; Pathways to Personal Growth*. Edinburgh: Floris books.

Sherwood, P. (2010a.) *Holistic counselling: A New Vision for Mental Health*. Bunbury: Sophia Publications.

Sherwood, P. (2013) *Emotional Literacy for Adolescent Mental Health*. Melbourne: Acer.

# CHAPTER 7
# Suicide Ideation

*"Killers aren't always assassins.*
*Sometimes, they don't even have blood on their hands."*

Ruta Sepetys (2019)

Suicide is defined as non accidental death due to inflicted self-harm that leads to death. The suicide rate per 100,000 in Australia was reported as 12.2% in 2018 with the largest concentration in the 30 to 59 age group (54.8%) followed by young people. In 2018 suicide accounted for 38.4% of deaths in the 15-24 age cohort. Males are three times more likely to commit suicide than females and it is the 10th leading cause of death for males and the 23rd leading cause of death for females. (ABS data, 2019). Indigenous suicides particularly in the Kimberley region of Western Australia are extremely high. A 2016 report found that the Kimberley suicide rate was seven times that of the rest of Australia and that 90% of suicides involved Indigenous people particularly youths, with a child as young as ten years of age committing suicide (Hondras, 2019). Crushing poverty, violence, addiction and abuse are endemic factors in these communities.

Behind these statistics are heartbroken families, communities and loved ones who continue to live with the grief and loss over decades. For parents it is an inestimable loss often accompanied by feelings of guilt, shame and despair as well as self-recrimination and resentment. There are high levels of stigma and blaming within families which often results in the need to conceal the loved one's cause of death. The resultant secrecy can become burdensome for the family and prevent members seeking help (Kučukalić & Kučukalić 2017). Compounded with this secrecy, are intense feelings of guilt or feelings of responsibility for the death and much rumination about "if only" someone or something else had been done to assist the person which prevents the grief from being processed or integrated. Rumination, obsessive preoccupation with the suicide and emotional stress contribute to complicated grief (CG) explicated by Shear (2012) as follows:

> (a)... painful and debilitating condition...characterized by prolonged, acute grief and complicating psychological features such as self-blaming thoughts and excessive avoidance of reminders of the loss." Conversely, instead of avoiding reminders of the deceased, some SB (suicide bereaved) people may "spend long periods of time trying to feel closer to the deceased through pictures, keepsakes, clothing, or other items associated with the loved one."

Complicated grief can afflict the survivors so that they are unable to function normally in their work or family life and may even contemplate suicide themselves. They may suffer from a range of psychosomatic disorders including poor sleep, loss of appetite and low energy (Spillane et al., 2018).

Family systems may become fractured as a result of a suicide, and marital breakups are more common following a suicide as are breakdowns and deterioration in family relationships. The severity is worse when the victim is young, particularly a teenager because the loss of the potential of a human being just about to enter their prime is indigestible (Flynn and Robinson, 2008). Such family members are also at greater risk for mental health disorders themselves following a suicide.

It is imperative that every effort is made in the delivery of mental health services to prevent suicide ideation moving to suicide. Extensive efforts are made during mental health week with campaigns like "RU ok?," to forestall suicides and to heighten community members' awareness of the signs of vulnerability in their family, friends and neighbours. Legg and Brazier (2018) outline indicators that show that a person could be experiencing suicidal thoughts;

- feeling intolerable emotional pain
- having or appearing to have an abnormal preoccupation with violence, dying, or death
- having mood swings, either happy or sad
- talking about revenge, guilt, or shame
- being agitated, or in a heightened state of anxiety
- experiencing changes in personality, routine, or sleeping patterns
- consuming drugs or more alcohol than usual, or starting drinking when they had not previously done so
- engaging in risky behaviour, such as driving carelessly or taking drugs
- getting their affairs in order and giving things away
- getting hold of a gun, medications, or substances that could end a life
- experiencing depression, panic attacks, impaired concentration
- increased isolation
- talking about being a burden to others
- psychomotor agitation, such as pacing around a room, wringing one's hands, and removing items of clothing and putting them back on

- saying goodbye to others as if it were the last time
- seeming to be unable to experience pleasurable emotions from normally pleasurable life events such as eating, exercise, social interaction, or sex
- severe remorse and self criticism
- talking about suicide or dying, expressing regret about being alive or ever having been born

While the causes of suicide ideation are varied, triggers include a sudden and overwhelming financial crisis, a relationship breakdown or divorce, prolonged unemployment or sudden redundancy, loss of children or a familial experience that leaves the person feeling alone, unsupported and unable to cope with the change. Change processes are always difficult but if they strike at the heart of an individual's most vulnerable area, where they have invested their life purpose and meaning whether it be family, work, career or children, then they are at higher risk for suicide ideation. Other risk factors include a personal or family history of mental health issues, addiction, violence, suicide together with feelings of hopelessness, loneliness and worthlessness. Compounding factors include substance abuse, psychiatric disorders, sleep deprivation, criminal charges portending, and lack of family support. All of the following mental health conditions are known to increase suicidal ideation (Legg and Brazier, 2018):

- adjustment disorder
- anorexia nervosa
- bipolar disorder
- body dysmorphic disorder
- borderline personality disorder
- dissociative identity disorder

- gender dysphoria, or gender identity disorder
- major depressive disorder
- panic disorder
- post-traumatic stress disorder (PTSD)
- schizophrenia
- social anxiety disorder
- generalized anxiety disorder
- substance abuse
- exposure to suicidal behaviour in others

Essentially, when dealing with a client expressing suicidal ideation, it is of course a responsible and essential part of the therapy that the level of risk is assessed and appropriate support structures and checks are in place prior to commencing sandplay. In addition, this includes ensuring that they have support either from their family or a close friend or acquaintance that can check in on them daily. This also involves encouraging the client to exercise, eat regularly and sleep at least eight hours per day. Referral to a medical practitioner and self-help groups would be part of the professional support offered to them. Providing them with emergency counselling support and a telephone number to call for help is critical, so that they have twenty four hour, seven day a week access to talk to a supportive, qualified person if they feel the need. Given this frontline work, it may then be appropriate to commence sandplay sessions as part of a comprehensive intervention to support the person with suicidal ideation, and help them to step further along in their journey to overcome trauma and create meaning in their lives.

## 1. Sandtray sequence for diagnosing the severity of the suicidal ideation.

It is not uncommon for adolescents to say that "I want to die" after a challenge or problem or crisis in their life. Adolescents live in a black and white world so life is often great or terrible, euphoric or tragic depending on the day's events as they move from one emotion to another, or one increasingly complex experience to another. Today, due to the social hypervigilence around adolescence and suicide ideation, people can sometimes over-react to what is only a bad day and a metaphoric way of speaking by an adolescent who says "I just want to die". This needs to be distinguished from a similar comment which is backed by the serious intention to take their life. Sandplay is extremely useful applied diagnostically here, as rather than talk to the adolescent, one can gain considerable insight into the adolescent's deeper psyche through sandplay. It is most important to ask the adolescent or adult who has said "I want to die" or "I am going to kill myself" to make a sandplay of how they are feeling. The two sand trays below illustrate the two possible outcomes: one that would flag a serious suicidal intention and one which would not be serious. Tray one demonstrates that diagnostically the therapist should be very concerned about such a statement as the client is at "high risk". Tray two shows a typical sand tray when the client is actually at "low-risk", despite what they may have said verbally.

### Step 1

- Ask the client to choose pieces to represent their feelings when they think about "killing themselves" in relation to their life now.

### Step 2

- Invite the client to describe what the pieces represent covering the following questions:

which piece represents yourself?

which pieces represent bad things/ persons in your life ( if any)

which pieces represent positive things/ persons in your life (if any)

which pieces represent your future? ( if any)

which pieces represent your past? ( if any)

which pieces represent the now?

which pieces represent the unknown? (if any)

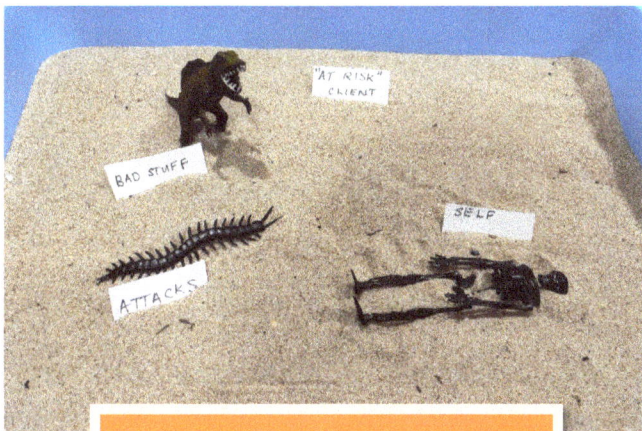

Image 28 (1a): high risk sandtray

## Reflection:

This image 28 (1a.) represents the sandplay of an "at risk" adolescent. There are no positive figurines in the sandtray at all. The client has no positive resources, and there is no indication of any future. The past is full of bad stuff and the present full of attacks that they have experienced from family and friends. The piece representing self is horizontal and lifeless.

In contrast sandplay 29 (1b) below, represents a low risk client despite their verbal protestations of wanting to kill themself.

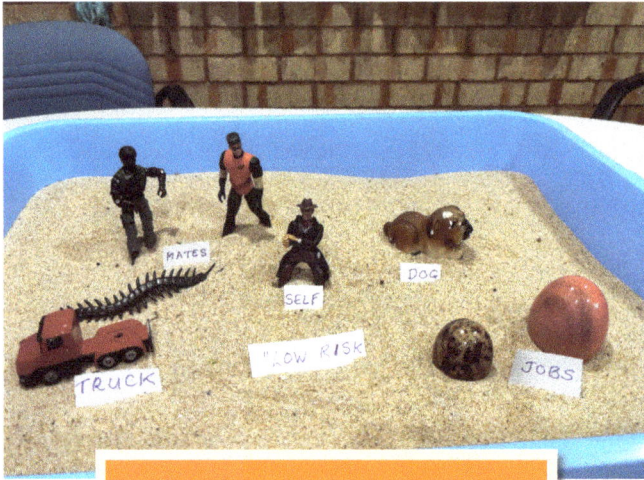

Image 29 (1b): low risk sandtray

Here, although the centipede represents the negative comments from his mates and the recent fight he has had with them, his self is central to the tray indicating strength to deal with his life challenges. The dog is seen as a positive resource in his life and the truck represents his desire to get his license and own his own vehicle. He wants to find work as a truckie. The eggs represent jobs he wants to obtain after finishing the school year. Here we have a client that has resources to deal with his current negative experience with his mates, as well as a vision of where he hopes to be in the future in terms of his life and employment. Despite this client saying that "he wants to kill himself" after a fight with his mates, the psyche's substructure revealed in the sand play, demonstrates that his life has a positive future and present resources. This diagnostic sandplay process provides the therapist with some psychotherapeutic depth to access the suicide risk of the client, together with other relevant instruments and assessments.

## 2. Making overt the suicide process to the client that has attempted suicide.

This sandplay sequence is used when clients have previously attempted suicide one or more times. The client is invited to choose objects and place them from left to right along the horizontal mid line of the sandtray:

### Step 1

- Ask the client to choose a piece to represent their feelings when they had the first thoughts about wanting to die and kill themself and place it in the sand tray. For example: "I have been dumped by my girlfriend and I want to die". It is placed in the mid line of the tray on the far left and labelled, "negative thoughts/feelings".

### Step 2

- Invite the client to choose a piece for the sand tray which represents their desire to escape from this world by dying and place it in the tray next to the last piece going across the tray from left to right and label it "escaping."

### Step 3

- Ask the client to choose a piece that represents how they feel just before the suicide attempt. It is placed in the tray next to the last piece going across the mid line of the tray and labelled by the client, "feeling just before the attempt."

### Step 4

- Ask the client to choose a piece that represents how they felt as they were attempting to take their own life. It is placed in the tray next to the last piece going across the mid line of the tray from left to right and is labelled, the "attempt".

## Step 5

- Invite the client to choose a piece to represent how they were feeling in the longer term after the suicide attempt. It is placed in the tray next to the last piece going across the mid line of the tray and labelled by the client "after the attempt."

Image 30: the after attempted suicide sequence

## Reflection:

Create a conversational space for the client if they wish to share experiences, or comment on the above. Once a trusting, nonjudgmental relationship is established with the client, then they may feel free to speak about the experience. When speaking about the images, they are likely to reveal deep traumas in their life that have led them to the suicide attempt as they have some concrete images to help them focus upon. Out of this conversation, in the next directed sandplay, we explore more deeply the nature of the "kill yourself" voice.

## 3. Sequence exposing the roots of the experiences and feelings of the " kill yourself" thoughts

### Step 1

- Ask the client to sense into the thoughts and feelings that they have, that drives them to attempt suicide.

### Step 2:

- Invite the client to select pieces to represent these thoughts and feelings.

### Step 3:

- Suggest that the client places these pieces in relation to a figurine representing their self.

- Label each piece clearly so they are easily identifiable.

Image 31: the feelings behind the "kill yourself" act

### Reflection:

In reflection with the client, note the trigger incidents in the client's experience that lead to each of these feelings. Work with the trigger incidents individually and over as many sessions as required by exploring further in sandplay how each one of these trigger feelings work in the client's life. Use a range of additional techniques to transform these negative feelings based upon one's clinical therapeutic model. Note the position of the self first, and if it is very weak, off-centre or crushed, begin by strengthening the "self" by bringing in some supportive figures that can be resources for the client. Also have the client identify which of these feelings behind the desire to give up on life, is the most dominant and pervasive. This becomes the core incident and the arena in which therapeutic interventions would make the most difference to the client's desire to live or die.

Do not begin this process until the client has become sufficiently motivated to desire to be able to state specific intentions to improve their feelings and the situation. This may involve considerable time spent finding a reason for the client to want to live and enlarging it sufficiently with the client so that it can become a raft back to life. Children, loved ones, pets, or a deeply respected person can be sources for providing this life-raft.

**Interventions:**

As a somatic therapist, one would undertake the following process for each of the negative qualities the client has placed in the above sandplay:

- Find where precisely in their body they feel the tension when speaking about a specific experience of one of their negative feelings eg. Failure

- Sense into this place and draw the shape of the tension

- Step into this place in the full body gesture of the shape that they have drawn

- Recall the earliest memory of sensing their body in this shape and the associated feelings

- How did the client feel? Attacked or abandoned or both? (In the case of feeling a failure, the most likely response is the feeling of attack through criticism)

- When the client has experienced being attacked, particularly when it comes as accumulated criticism and judgment from others, it is important to remove the force of the judgment attack. In holistic counselling the compassion triangle sequence is ideal as identified in Sherwood (2013 pp.40-41). Then follow by implementing protective boundary exercises.

Once having addressed, over a number of sessions, the qualities identified in the above sandplay the therapist would proceed to the following directed sand play.

## 4. Sandplay sequence for identifying the missing qualities required by the client to prevent them moving from feeling negative to attempting suicide.

**Step 1:**

- Invite the client to select pieces to represent the qualities which would prevent them attempting suicide that is what are the positive qualities missing in their life and ask them to place these pieces in the sandtray.

**Step 2:**

- Ask the client to select a piece representing themself and place in the sand tray and then place the other pieces in relation to themself.

- Suggest the client place the most important pieces closer to the figurine representing them self. In this example, love was by far the most important quality, followed by understanding and being valued.

**Image 32: the positive feelings that prevent a suicide attempt**

## Reflection:

Discuss the implications of these qualities for the client's life. Follow up with the client the identified new qualities that need to come into their life in order for them not to need to progress to a suicide attempt and in order to feel that life is worth living. This will involve a number of internal changes for the client's thinking life as well as external changes such as networking, support mentoring, establishing new opportunities in social, sporting or educational contexts. Work with each of the qualities in the sandtray, so as to create a space for the client to embody each quality in their lives through a particular activity. Engage family, school and other support networks when and where relevant. Invite the client to photograph the sand tray containing these new possibilities and to refer to it regularly for the following seven days.

At this point, the therapist can reinforce that a basic resourcing exercise is essential. It consists of receiving the quality from a positive image, breathing it into their body where it is needed, becoming the gesture of the quality, finding a sound or song for the quality and drawing, painting , making in clay or otherwise creating an embodied form that represents the flow of that positive quality into their life. This process is enumerated in Sherwood, (2008,p.98). If there are visible blocks to any one of these qualities then further sandplay and /or somatic work would be undertaken to address the trauma underlying the blockage to the new healing quality.

## 5. Sandplay sequence: creating the vision of what is the positive potential of their life to prevent a return to suicidal ideation.

### Step 1:

- Invite the client to place a figurine representing themself in the tray that represents self-acceptance of their limitations and strengths.

### Step 2:

- Suggest that the client select figurines that represent the potential of their life and place them around the self-accepting figure.

### Step 3 :

- Suggest that the client photograph the completed sequence as a reminder of the positive potential of their life and their acceptance of their strengths and limitations in the world.

Image 33: finding self-acceptance and the positive potential of their life

## Reflection:

Open a conversational space for the client to share experiences of self-acceptance and the challenges to it. Enlarge the opportunities for the client to experience contact with support networks that promote these positive qualities that support the client's vision of their future.

Sandplay sequences provide powerful pictures to create new visions of positive pathways and meaningful reasons for living in the world. Combined with embodied strategies that embrace the expressive therapies such as music, art making, equine therapy and pet therapy which are documented in Sherwood (2013), there is real hope through this process of positively re-engaging these clients on a path to meaningful renewal within themselves and in their lives.

## REFERENCES

ABS (2019) *Suicide facts and stats* from  Australian Bureau of Statistics (ABS) Catalogue 3303.0 Cause of Death Australia,

2018 released in September 2019. Cited in Life in mind  https://www.
lifeinmindaustralia.com.au/about-suicide/suicide-data/suicide-facts-
and-stats Accessed 4-1-20.

Flynn L, Robinson E. (2008) Family issues in suicide postvention.
Australian Institute of Family Studies. *AFRC Briefing No. 8* (February
2008). https://aifs.gov.au/cfca/publications/family-issues-suicide-
postvention. Accessed 4-1-2020.

Harris, T., & Molock S (2010) Cultural Orientation, Family Cohesion,
and Family Support in *Suicide Ideation and Depression among African
American College Students.*  Wiley online library

https://doi.org/10.1111/j.1943-278X.2000.tb01100.x

Hondras, N. (2019)  *If the Kimberly was a country it would have the worst
suicide rate in the world.* https://www.watoday.com.au/national/
western-australia/if-the-kimberley-was-a-country-it-would-
have-the-worst-suicide-rate-in-the-world-20190207-p50wem.html
Accessed 4-1-2020.

Kučukalić S, Kučukalić A. (2017) Stigma and suicide. *Psychiatr Danub.*
2017; 29(Suppl 5):895-899.

Legg, T., & Brazier, Y (2018 What are suicidal thoughts? *Medical news
today*  https://www.medicalnewstoday.com/articles/193026.php
Accessed 4-1-2020.

Sepetys, R., (2019) *Salt to the Sea*  https://www.goodreads.com/
quotes/tag/trauma. Accessed 24-12-2019.

Shear MK. (2012) Grief and mourning gone awry: pathway and course
of complicated grief. *Dialogues Clin Neurosci.* 2012; 14(2):119-128.

Sherwood, P (2013) *Emotional Literacy for Adolescent Mental Health*
Melbourne: Acer.

Sherwood, P. (2008) *Emotional Literacy: the Heart of classroom
management* Melbourne; Acer.

Spillane A, Matvienko-Sikar K, Larkin C, Corcoran P, Arensman E. (2018) *What are the physical and psychological health effects of suicide bereavement on family members? An observational and interview mixed-methods study in Ireland. BMJ Open.* 2018;8(1). https://bmjopen.bmj.com/content/8/1/e019472?cpetoc=&int_source=trendmd&int_medium=trendmd&int_campaign=trendmd  Accessed 14-1-2020.

 Yasgur, B (2018) Those Left Behind: Working With Suicide-Bereaved Families. In *Psychiatry Advisor* https://www.psychiatryadvisor.com/home/topics/suicide-and-self-harm/those-left-behind-working-with-suicide-bereaved-families/

## CHAPTER 8
# Divorce

*Divorce is one of the most destructive, emotionally traumatic experiences a human being can go through, no matter if you're the instigator or the recipient. It's hard, and it hurts, and it takes a long time to feel normal again."*

Emily V.Gordon (2020)

D ivorce is a legal process for ending a legal marriage. The total number of divorces in Australia has been declining over the past decade from 2.7 per thousand people to 2.1 per thousand people and marriages have been lasting longer with a movement from 10.7 years to 12.1 years (McCrindle, 2020). In 2017, it was only 2 per 1000 persons. The number of divorces involving children is now 47.1%, also on the decline (AIFS, 2020).

However, this data does not reflect the entire situation due to the escalating number of couples living in "defacto" relationships. There are many unrecorded "breakups" among defacto relationships. There is an increasing number of family systems with children from more than two fathers and parents engaged in balancing unresolved trauma from multiple "de facto" breakups. Statistics do not capture the number of de-facto relationship endings, as many persons do not file for assets or custody of the children but simply move on or out, particularly when the relationship has lasted less than two years. There are an increasing number of children presenting in therapy in this category, suffering the trauma of abandonment or rejection by one parent, and deprived economic, housing and educational access and often with step-siblings with whom they have to compete for attention and resources. The feminization of poverty, first identified by Diana Pearce (1978) which refers to the higher ratio of women compared to men living in poverty has continued, and is exacerbated by divorces and de-facto relationship breakdowns where single mother families disproportionately bear the cost of child raising (Mc Lanahan & Carlson, 2001).

Divorce has a number of traumatic side effects and nowhere is it more clearly demonstrated than in relation to suicide. The data shows that persons who are divorced or separated have a 2.4 times greater risk of suicide than married persons. Kposowa (2003) cited in Sullivan (2019), identified differences between the suicide rates among divorced men, as compared to divorced women. Divorced men were nine times more likely to die by suicide than divorced women. In therapy it is generally recognized that men in general cope far less well emotionally with divorce than women, and are more likely to be surprised or unprepared for divorce even when the woman has told them many times prior to the divorce that she is planning on leaving if certain things in the relationship do not change or are not addressed. Therefore, these men suffer from an intense shock of disbelief, disorientation and despair. Even years later after the divorce has been completed, many men still harbour the notion that their ex-wife will come back to them at some time in their future.

Vitelli (2015) noted that the number of consequences from a divorce include financial, psychological, social and health. Psychological issues include increased stress, lower life satisfaction and depression, to which should be added grief and loss, emotional challenges in maintaining an ongoing relationship with their children, loss of in-law family members, friends and loss of acquaintances. For some persons the fear of social judgment and / or rejection or ridicule is very high, particularly in more traditional cultures or conservative religions. Women who have developed an identity which is primarily focused as carer around the family, find that a divorce can be particularly devastating.

Vitelli (2015) also noted that research found that divorced couples suffered from increased medical visits, and an overall increase in mortality risk compared to those who remain married. Single persons do not have the same support networks to act as a buffer against stresses created financially, at work or in their social activities. Although the "no-fault" Divorce Act passed in Australia in 1975, has removed the stressors of legally blaming and "dirt collecting" against the other person, divorce still remains at the personal and social level a time for self and other recriminations, judgments and re-assessments. Even after the legal paperwork has been completed, the emotional fall-out continues for years, particularly when children are involved and joint custody or custody access is in place.

Abrams (2019) lists a range of post-traumatic stress symptoms that may follow a divorce for some people which include:

- Overly negative thoughts about oneself or the world
- Exaggerated self-blame or blame of others
- Decreased interest in activities
- Feeling isolated
- Irritability or aggression
- Paranoia
- Risky or destructive behavior
- Difficulty concentrating
- Difficulty sleeping.

However, when divorces have been accompanied by bitterness, violence or revenge then more serious trauma is the resultant. Coleman cited in Abrams (2019) identifies that PTSD or post- traumatic stress disorder can have its roots in divorces which have been physically or emotionally abusive and/or in which the divorce process is particularly acrimonious, drawn out and/ or accompanied by threats of physical violence, injury or death against one party by another, or against their children.

Consequently, the types of interventions one would do in a sandplay vary depending on the level of stress and anxiety of the presenting person. Below are four directed sandplay sequences that are suitable for a variety of persons as they work on building their resilience and helping themself to move to step forward into a new life.

### 1. Sandplay sequence for facilitating a client moving on from a partner after a divorce and reclaiming themself.

Most people who have been in a committed marriage under-estimate the emotional and psychological dynamics of moving on and "letting go" in relation to their previous spouse, particularly if the relationship has been long term, that has exceeded five years or they have experienced betrayal. Their focus will be on the negative experiences that have brought about the divorce and their decision to leave or their abandonment by their spouse. Too often the client forgets the intense emotional and psychological enmeshment between themselves and their ex-partner. This first sequence is called "reclaiming the parts of one-self".

**Step 1**

- Ask the client to choose a piece to represents themself and to place in the sandtray.

**Step 2**

- Invite the client to choose a figurine that represents their ex-partner/ ex-spouse and place it in the sandtray.

**Step 3**

- Ask the client to list down all the parts of their life they have given their partner. For example, their love, their sexuality, their finances, their home-making, their loyalty, their heart and write these down on slips of paper.

**Step 4**

- Ask the client to choose figurines that represent each one of these qualities and place them around the ex-partner.

**Step 5**

- Invite the client to dissolve all "vows, promises, contracts" ever made to their ex-partner to allow the ex-partner to access these parts of themself by speaking out loud as follows: "I hereby dissolve all vows, promises, contracts I have ever made with you to take responsibility for your well being in any way. I set you free to be responsible for your own well being and I set myself free to be responsible for my own well being."

**Step 6**

- Invite the client to call back all of the parts of themself while speaking out loud: "I hereby call back all parts of myself I have given you including my"… name the parts in the sandplay.

- As the client names each part they move it close to the figurine of themself, taking it away from their ex-partner.

- Invite the client to repeat out loud: "I set my self free to be responsible for my own well-being and I set my ex-partner free to be responsible for their own well being."

- Ask the client if they wish to now create a boundary between themself and their reclaimed parts and their ex-partner.

**Image 34: reclaiming oneself: parts given away**

**Image 35: reclaiming oneself: reclaiming one's parts**

## Reflection:

Spend time with the client reflecting on their feelings in completing this reclaiming of their parts process. Do they feel it is complete?

Where did they feel blocks or difficulties if any? Are there any changes in their behaviour that they would wish to make, given the insights that have emerged in this sequence? Out of this conversation usually the second directed sandplay sequence will arise either in the same or next counselling session.

## 2. Sequence in relation to moving on after divorce: releasing the ex-partner.

### Step 1

- Ask the client to choose a piece to represents themself and place it in the sandtray.

### Step 2:

- Ask the client to choose a figurine that represents their ex-partner and place it in the sandtray.

### Step 3:

- Invite the client to list down all the parts that their ex-partner gave to them, or they have taken and that they feel they still have in some way. For example, their love, their sexuality, their finances, their home-making, their loyalty, their heart, their emotions and write these down on slips of paper.

- Suggest the client choose figurines to represent each of these parts and place them in the sand tray around their self.

### Step 4:

- Suggest the client repeat out loud that "I hereby return to you all parts of you that I have in my possession still." The client names each piece as they return these to their ex-partner by moving them away from the self and around the ex-partner.

- Invite the client to place a boundary around them self while repeating out loud: "You no longer have any emotional or energetic access to me, nor I to you."

- Suggest the client repeat at the conclusion: "I set you free to be responsible for your own well being and I set myself free to be responsible for my own well-being".

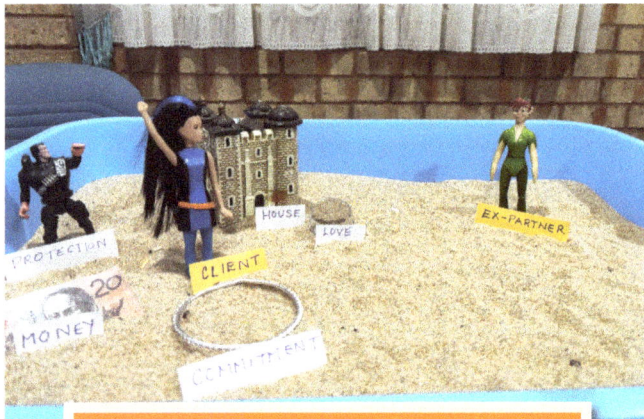

**Image 36: releasing the ex-partner: parts he has given or you have taken**

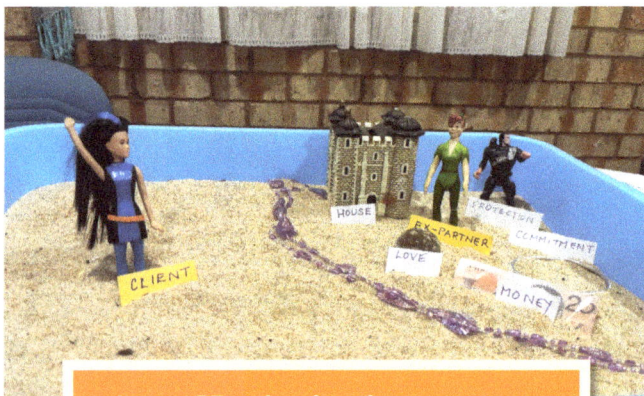

**Image 37: releasing the ex-partner: returning ex-partner's parts**

## Reflection:

In reflection with the client assess how they are feeling. Are they at peace? Agitated? Angry or in grief and loss? Do they feel the separation is complete? Where did they feel blocks or difficulties if any? Are there any changes in their behaviour that they would wish to make, given the insights that have emerged in this sequence? Out of this conversation usually further sandtrays would be completed to process the grief and loss, the anger, feelings of betrayal and/or distress. Usually these will be largely spontaneous sandplays, rather than directed sandplay sequences.

## 3. Sandplay sequence for resourcing the absent father.

Usually children are in grief and loss over the parents' divorce except where there has been violence and/or sexual abuse in the family system. They do not wish to be alienated from either parent in the majority of cases and experience grief and loss in relation to their family breakup and in particular in relation to the parent that they now see rarely, infrequently or not at all. There are an increasing number of children, particularly from short term "de-facto" relationships, who no longer see their fathers and live in a chronic state of longing. Most children from divorced situations when given a magic wand and asked if they had one wish to change anything in their life what would it be, respond: "to have Mum and Dad together again." (This of course excludes most children from violent or sexually abusive family systems). The following sand play sequence is to assist children to cope with the absent father.

## Step 1:

- Invite the child/ adolescent to list down all the qualities of their father that they miss, whether real or hoped for.

**Step 2:**

- Ask the client to select a piece that represents them and to place it in the sandtray.

- Invite the client to select pieces that represent all of the qualities of a father that they have listed down and place these around themself.

- Suggest that for each piece the child breathes it into their body and tells a story about when they experienced that feeling last in their life.

**Step 3:**

- Ask the child to place next to that quality anyone else or anything else that reminds them of that quality.

- If they cannot think of anyone or anything, then suggest possibilities with the client.

- However if the client does not respond to these then leave the space empty in the tray.

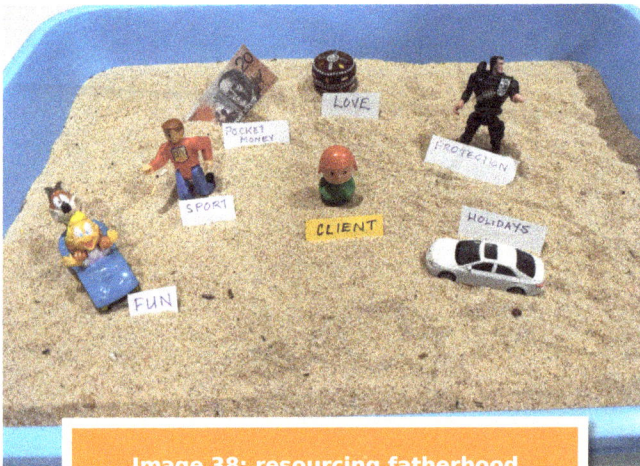

**Image 38: resourcing fatherhood**

**Reflection:**

Follow up with the client the identified new qualities that need to come into their lives in order for the them to be able to receive these qualities in different ways now that their father is absent or they do not see him frequently. This will involve a number of internal changes for the client's thinking life as well as external changes such as networking, support mentoring, establishing new opportunities in social, sporting or educational contexts. Work with each of the qualities in the sandtray so as to create a space for the client to embody each quality in their lives through a particular activity. Engage family, school and other support networks when and where required. Invite the client to photograph the sand tray containing these new possibilities and to refer to it regularly, especially when they feel sad about not being able to see their father.

## 4. Sandplay: restoring the qualities of motherhood.

As children and youth of divorced parents are more likely to end up with their mother or spending more time with their mother, the issue may often be that they feel that they no longer have the same attention from their mother who is pre-occupied with making a living and running a household alone. The need for this sequence is indicated whenever a child expresses that they feel the need for more of the qualities of motherhood. The mother has already been addressed regarding her capacity to provide these or otherwise.

**Step 1:**

- Invite the child/ youth to place a figurine representing themself in the centre of the tray

**Step 2:**

- Suggest the client makes a list of all the qualities of their mother that they would like or qualities of their mother of which they would like more.

## Step 3:

- Invite the client to select figurines that represent each of these qualities and place them around the figurine representing themself.

## Step 4:

- Ask the client to step inside each figurine imaginatively and choose a piece to represent a time when they have experienced that feeling in their life from someone or something other than their mother.

- Photograph the completed sequence as a reminder of the resources that they can access in their lives.

Image 39: resourcing motherhood

## Reflection:

Follow up with the client the identified new qualities that need to come into their lives in order for the child/youth to receive these qualities in different ways now that their mother is no longer as available as they would like, to give them these qualities. This will involve a number of internal changes for the child/adolescent's thinking life as well as external changes such as networking, support mentoring, establishing new opportunities in social, sporting or educational contexts. Work with each of the qualities in the sandtray so as to create a space for the client to embody each quality in their lives through a particular activity. Engage family, school and other support networks when and where required. Invite the client to use the photograph of the sand tray in their daily life as required.

## Dealing with fear and anxiety

Whenever a client manifests fear and anxiety, the therapist should not commence with sandplay at all, but rather begin by diagnosing the level of fear and then commence to have the client find three resources that could protect them from their fear and teach the client how to "ground" and be present in the present moment. Educate a client to recognise how fear arises in the body in one part and then spreads all over the body if left unaddressed. The first strategy would be teaching the client how to exit the fear and anxiety by using a somatic sequence that enables exiting the fear or trauma. This is detailed in Sherwood (2008, p.78). It was developed by Tagar and is also documented in Sherwood (2010, p.43). This simple sequence is very calming and restores the breathing prior to commencing any other therapeutic work around the fear.

Bamboo sequence - Exiting client from immediate panic/fear/shaking.

1. Where in the body do you feel the fear?
2. Collect the fear with your hands as if you are taking away a ball of fear. Throw the ball of fear as far away from you making a loud "earth" sound i.e. 'g' 'b' 'd'.
3. Step backwards and stamp your feet firmly and loudly.

4.   While stamping your feet shake your hands to remove all fear.

5.   Repeat out loud: "I am here, I am safe, I am protected".

Repeat steps one to five above for at least five times or more, until breathing is regular and fear has gone.

### 5. Sandplay: protecting the client from the fear of attack.

The client is now able to complete a basic sandplay sequence on protecting themselves against their fear.

**Step 1:**

•   Invite the child/ youth to place a piece in the tray, representing themself as the wounded one that has been attacked, in the tray

**Step 2:**

•   Suggest the client selects figurines or a figurine to represent the forces attacking them which they experience as the force of the fear attacking them, leaving them feeling twisted, scrunched, stabbed, poked squashed, flattened etc.

**Step 3:**

•   Invite the client to place a figurine that represents a strong guard that can protect them, and place it between themself and the force attacking them.

•   Invite the client to add anything else protective such as another protector or a boundary that they experience as protecting them from the attacking force.

**Step 4:**

•   Suggest the client breathe in the power of the guard to protect them and take a photograph of it. They can refer to the guard daily for at least seven days and whenever they feel fear arising within themself.

Image 40: protecting the fearful one from the attacking force

## Reflection:

Follow up with the client on the importance of visualising a guard standing between themselves and their fear. The importance of not being alone in the face of fear is emphasized. Encourage them to visualise the guard around them, and to find a song that represents the power of their chosen guard to protect them. To actually remove the foundational cause of the fear, that is the initial incident that is triggering the client into recurrent fear, it may not be skilful to use sandplay. A somatically based sequence of enter-exit-behold or empowerment sequence as previously described would give the client insight without the risk of flooding. It would also enable them to transform the fear without being overwhelmed by it (Sherwood, 2010, pp141-144).

In summary, divorce brings many of a person's unresolved traumas to the surface and opens literally a "can of worms" for the members of the family system. Many books have been written upon it and the above are only a few adjunct exercises developed in sandplay to address some of the traumas that the divorcing process unleashes. Lockhart (2019) captures the trauma of the divorce experience when he states: "Divorce shreds the muscles of our hearts so that they will hardly beat without a struggle".

## REFERENCES

Abrams, A., (2019) Post divorce trauma and PTSD.  In *Verywell Mind* https://www.verywellmind.com/post-divorce-trauma-4583824 Accessed 10-1-2020.

AIFS (2020) Divorce rates in Australia https://aifs.gov.au/facts-and-figures/divorce-rates-australia. Accessed 10-1-2020.

Dreman, S (1991) Coping with the trauma of divorce. In *Journal of Traumatic Stress* 4, 113–121(1991).

Gordon, E., (2020) http://www.quoteambition.com/divorce-quotes-sayings/  Accessed 6-1-2020.

Lockhart, E., (2019) *We Were Liars* https://www.goodreads.com/quotes/tag/divorce-separation-children.  Accessed 6-1-2020.

Mc Lanahan, S., & Carlson, M., (2001) Poverty and gender in affluent nations. In *International Encyclopedia of the Social and Behavioural Sciences.* https://www.sciencedirect.com/topics/psychology/feminization-of-poverty.  Accessed 6-1-2020.

McCrindle, M., (2020) **https://aifs.gov.au/facts-and-figures/divorce-rates-australia**. Accessed 6-1-2020.

Pearce, D. (1978). The feminization of poverty: Women, work and welfare. In Urban *and Social Change Review, 11*, 28–36.

Sherwood, P. (2008) *Emotional Literacy: the Heart of classroom management* Melbourne; Acer.

Sherwood, P (2010) *Holistic Counselling: a New Vision of Mental Health.* Bunbury; Sophia Publications.

Sullivan G. (2019) Divorce Is a Risk Factor for Suicide, Especially for Men. In *Psychology Today* https://www.psychologytoday.com/us/ blog/acquainted-the-night/201906/divorce-is-risk-factor-suicide-especially-men accessed 6-1-2020.

Vitelli, R. (2015) Life after divorce. In *Psychology Today* https://www. psychologytoday.com/us/blog/media-spotlight/201507/life-after-divorce. Accessed 6-1-2020.

# Conclusion

Complex and challenging mental health conditions such as addiction, obsessive compulsive disorder, traumatic mutism, anorexia, cutting, body dysmorphia and suicide ideation can often afflict the life of the sufferer and adversely affect their families for many years. They are therapeutically complicated and challenging particularly when they have progressed over years. To infer that sandplay alone, however skilfully and innovatively implemented, can cure these conditions would be misleading to say the least.

While the empirical research is limited on the efficacy of sandplay for these conditions, my clinical practice over many clients does demonstrate that experientially, clients' symptoms when undertaking these directed sand play sequences reduce, and in some cases disappear entirely. However, it is more realistic to combine the directed sandplay techniques presented in this book with additional psychotherapeutic interventions based on the therapist's model of training.

The directed sandplay techniques in this book, however, do embrace a number of evidence based strategies. They are diagnostic sequences such as explicating what is running the addiction process or the body dysmorphia process. In fact, sandplay is extremely appropriate for diagnostic experiential investigations as it unveils layers of meaning in the client's experience. There is also much use of guided image making across all of the mental health issues presented herein. Sandplay enables the use of concrete objects, the figurines, to represent emotional states and as such is particularly effective in creating guided image making exercises.

As an extension of this, the sandplay process also facilitates cognitive restructuring and reframing in an extremely concrete manner so that the client actually physically embodies through the movement of the figurines in the sand tray, the cognitive restructuring and reframing process. Extensive use is made of this in all the directed sandplay techniques. The use of the client's mobile phone to photograph these completed reframed images is particularly helpful in the follow-up days allowing them to review the new image.

Social skills training is also incorporated in these directed sandplay sequences and is nowhere clearer than in the "speaking up sequence" in the chapter about traumatic mutism. The behavioural experiments are embedded in the directed sandplay process, as clients are encouraged to reframe their lives, and create new images of themself and their lives, with the previously missing qualities added. They are then asked to show using the figurines how this changes their perception of themself.

These directed sandplay sequences are also useful in facilitating the client's broadening perception of themself and the possibilities in their lives which promote relapse prevention and allow self-regulation, particularly if the client consistently visualises these changes on a daily basis.

Directed sandplay has the capacity to expose the client to the deeper level of psychological dynamics within themself, while simultaneously, through the use of figurines, distancing the client sufficiently so that they can experience exposure and desensitisation almost simultaneously. This enables the client to better digest, understand and assimilate the psychological dynamics within themself as they are revealed through the sand play.

These directed sandplay sequences contain the dynamics and core patterns that I have observed with many hundreds of clients during therapeutic processes. It is from these core patterns that the directed sandplay sequences have been constructed to economize on time, given the constraints of a limited number of clinical sessions available to any one client. These are shown in the hope that they might provide therapeutic adjuncts to recovery from these complex and otherwise debilitating mental health conditions.

Traumatic experiences embodied in a person are like indigestible food, invisible, irritating, inflaming and nauseating the person, particularly when triggered by contemporary experiences. The clinical work is to find and reintegrate these mostly unconscious traumas. These directed sandplay sequences, combined with somatic sequences outlined in this book offer a powerful pathway for client who has been traumatised to discover and re-integrate otherwise unknown and disturbing experiences into their life in a way that is both healing and empowering. Trauma survivors have an incredible capacity to heal given a safe, protective and supportive space. Van Der Kolk (2014, p.283) so brilliantly summarises this:

> Beneath the surface of the protective parts of trauma survivors there exists an undamaged essence, a Self that is confident, curious, and calm, a Self that has been sheltered from destruction by the various protectors that have emerged in their efforts to ensure survival. Once those protectors trust that it is safe to separate, the Self will spontaneously emerge, and the parts can be enlisted in the healing process.

May these directed sandplay sequences strengthen the self so that it may flourish, realise and come to manifest its highest potential as a human being.

## References:

Van Der Kolk, B. (2014) *The Body Keeps the Score: Brain, Mind, and Body in the Healing of Trauma* N.Y., Viking.

www.ingramcontent.com/pod-product-compliance
Lightning Source LLC
Chambersburg PA
CBHW041215030426
42336CB00023B/3350